CRY OF THE NORTHLAND

by Kenneth Eagle
as told to Virginia Crider

CHRISTIAN LIGHT PUBLICATIONS, INC.
Harrisonburg, Virginia 22801-1212

Christian Light Publications, Inc.
Harrisonburg, Virginia 22801-1212
© 1973 by Christian Light Publications, Inc.
All rights reserved. Published 1973
Printed in the United States of America
Third Printing, 1997

06 05 04 03 02 01 00 99 98 97   5 4 3 2 1

Cover by Martha Yoder

ISBN 0-87813-505-7

To
the many people who have labored
behind the scenes
at the Northern Light Gospel
Mission, but have received no recog-
nition, I dedicate
this book.
Kenneth Eagle

TABLE OF CONTENTS

INTRODUCTION

This book deals with the spiritual adventures of a flesh and blood individual, whom I have chosen to call Kenneth Eagle. The basic material is factual; however, in writing such a story, every event or conversation cannot be authentic in all of its details, and for various reasons a few incidents have been altered. Brother Eagle has checked the manuscript for basic accuracy, as have also officials of the Northern Light Gospel Mission.

All names are fictitious. Brother Eagle wishes to remain unidentified for a variety of reasons, all of them legitimate. We have honored his request.

Since the story is written in the first person, and since I have quoted Brother Eagle almost verbatim a number of times in order to preserve his unique style of expression, the publishers and I feel that his name should appear as co-author of the book, although he protests this.

The authors release this book with the prayer that it may bring honor and glory to God, and that many souls will be led into a deeper relationship with Him through reading its pages.

October 16, 1972   B.V.C.

I

INTO THE HILLS

From our living room window the hills loomed in the background, low, grey, and foreboding. Murderers, desperadoes, and outlaws took refuge in those hills. Rocks and boulders of every size littered their slopes, offering a hiding place from the authorities. Everyone in our village near Philadelphia knew the character of those hills; but for us, the Eagle family, our relationship to their rock-studded slopes was a much more personal thing.

From the time I can remember, my brother John and I had feared those hills. When we were very young, and unruly, as boys will be, Dad threatened, "Kenneth, John, boys who won't obey will be taken out into the hills." We cringed in fright. In our small minds the hills, the rocks, and the outlaws were synonymous.

When we became somewhat older, Dad took us on berry-picking expeditions into the hill area near Oberlin. We saw for ourselves the rocky woodlands, twisting roads, and hill residents.

"This is Murderer's Road," Dad had told us, as we drove along. "It's rightly named." Huge boulders bordered that road. Others of varying sizes were scattered among the trees. Here and there one rock lay atop another. Sometimes several large boulders were stacked together, the work of Nature's Architect.

"You see," Dad continued, twisting the steering wheel expertly as the road snaked among the boulders, "all kinds of people live in these hills. Thieves and murderers come here to hide from the cops." John and I peered fearfully at those huge rocks. A man could easily hide behind many of them. Dad laughed at our bulging, frightened eyes. "Bootleggers like this area, too," he added.

I could understand why outlaws found this country ideal for hiding out. Hunting a man in this jungle of rocks and woodland would be like searching for a four-leaf clover in five acres of lawn grass.

"That is Cousin Cass's lane," Dad announced, as we passed a narrow, rutted side-road. "You remember Cousin Cass, don't you?"

How could we possible forget her? Almost we expected to see

her dusty, chauffeur-driven white hearse creeping around the bend in the lane.

About every three months Dad's red haired cousin appeared in our village in the white hearse. It was replete with casket, flowers, and a derby hat for the driver. Instead of a body, the casket contained gallons of Cousin Cass's bootleg liquor.

In spite of its dusty appearance, some people were probably deceived by the vehicle, but the authorities knew Cousin Cass. She was arrested several times.

"Ha, ha, ha!" Cousin Cass chortled in our home after her release following a court hearing. "I fooled those cops today!"

"Why? What happened?" Dad had asked curiously, his cheroot dangling from the corner of his mouth.

Cousin Cass laughed uproariously. "They took me into court and asked me what I had done. I played it smart. I just said, 'I killed little cock robin.' I wouldn't say another word and they didn't have any evidence against me, so they let me go." Her escapades did bring Cousin Cass several prison terms, but she always returned to her old trade upon her release from jail.

Dad also pointed out the orchard of Old Apricot Alice. Although most of the hill residents had adopted the automobile for transportation, Apricot Alice peddled her fruit from door to door in the valley with horse and buggy. Nor was her transportation her only distinguishing characteristic. Scraggly hair, a snuff container, and foul language liberally interspersed with oaths characterized Apricot Alice.

On different occasions we had seen other hill people stumbling about drunk, tobacco juice dripping from their beards and chins. We had witnessed them carrying guns, prepared to take the law into their own hands. Our daily papers sometimes reported accounts of these shootouts.

We realized, of course, that people of reputable character must also populate these hills, but somehow we failed to see them!

My apprehension concerning the hill country and its populace stemmed from this knowledge. I knew even in those early years of my life the conditions existing in the unpainted shanties up and down those rock-strewn lanes.

Well, had it not been for the depression, my knowledge of the hills might never have become first-hand.

Unexpectedly, after thirteen years employment with the City Transit Company in Philadelphia, Dad came home with the shattering news that he had been laid off. Compared to what others were earning at the time, his pay had been good. We lived in a comfortable home. But now Dad's job was gone. No money would come in. We had no means whereby we could buy clothing, food, or fuel.

For some reason Dad had never lived for the future. He hadn't considered the possibility of misfortune. It had not occurred to him that the time might come when he would need a nest egg to see us through a national crisis. He had no savings tucked away to help us now.

I overheard Mother and Dad talking one memorable day. I was just a boy—twelve, perhaps—but even I could sense the seriousness of the situation.

"But if we move into the rocks," Dad insisted stubbornly, "living will be easier. We can have a garden and raise our own food. We can even cut our own fuel. And," he added hopefully, "maybe I can pick up some odd jobs and we can ride out this financial crisis."

Mother's voice trembled. I couldn't see her, but I knew she must be wringing her hands. "Oh, no, Ralph! We can't do that! We can't take our children into a place like that. Why, the people up there are terrible. And," Mother paused timidly, "the only kind of work most of them do is—is—" she rushed on, "bootlegging. You wouldn't want to do that, would you?" Dad didn't reply directly to Mother's question. Her tears flowed as he said, "Under the circumstances, we have no choice. We have to move to the hills, Susan."

Dad's decision shook Mother. Her family had been devout, church-going people. Faced with this move into the hills, Mother began to pray. I'm not sure just what she expected in response to her prayers, but I do know that she believed in God's faithfulness—although, in the years that followed—she must often have wondered if He had heard. She may even have forgotten the anguished cries of that period of her life. Nevertheless, the Lord did not forget.

Dad sold our car to pay moving expenses. The day came when a moving van pulled up to our door. All our worldly goods were loaded on, and out into the hills we went.

II

THE HILL HOME

How familiar those hills seemed as the bulky van twisted around the sharp bends in the winding road!

The first buds of spring were pushing from the trees, lending a faint greenish tinge to the woods. Here and there the red bloom of apples mingled with the greens, making a pleasing contrast. Small wild flowers, strangers to us, peeked shyly from among the rocks. It wasn't a bad place, I decided. Perhaps this move to the hills would turn out all right after all.

"I remember that rock!" John exclaimed. "See, Kenneth, it's our old elephant rock." The creases and seams in the boulder did resemble elephant ears.

"Here's the Devil's Potato Patch, boys," Dad motioned. "We'll soon be there, Mother." The "potato patch" consisted of an area made up entirely of small stones, much smaller than the majority of rocks found in the hill country. Many of these stones, when tapped, had a strange melodious ring.

"This is our lane," Dad announced. A narrow rutted road wound upward between stones which had been pushed aside to build the road. Those too large to shift had been dodged, causing tortuous twists. The lane emerged into a sunlit clearing. A small, unpainted house with a nearby barn and chicken house nestled in the cleared area. A weathered picket fence surrounded the house and garden.

The moving men dumped the furniture into the front room and departed. Mother looked about hopelessly. "Where will we put everything?" she asked dejectedly. "It's so small, Ralph!"

"We have four rooms and the attic," Dad answered. "We can store what we don't need there or in the barn. Later . . ."

"Later we'll have a better home?" Mother supplied. "I hope so, Ralph."

In the end the extra furniture went into one of the four rooms while John and I were delegated to the attic. We found we could lie on our backs and touch the eaves. The novelty of sleeping in the attic excited us.

Dad positioned the Royal Bride cook stove and set up the stove pipe. He took the ax and headed for the woods just beyond our yard. "There's plenty of wood lying out there,

Susan. I'll get some for you," he told Mother.

Mother sank into a chair. She looked at the bare board walls, the unceiled rooms, the ladder into the attic, the unpainted floors. Tears rushed to her eyes and dropped into her lap. She cried briefly.

"This won't do, boys!" she said, jumping to her feet. "Kenneth, here is the water bucket. Take Nancy and see if you can find the well. John, perhaps you can roll Vernon's crib into the bedroom and it will be out of the way. We'll get things put to rights as best we can, then get some lunch. We'll all feel better."

Five-year-old Nancy skipped along happily as we toured the yard, seeking the well. We discovered several boulders inside our fence. Nancy scrambled to the top of one. "Ooh, it's cold!" she squealed.

We found the well, a crank-operated affair, near the back door. A rope lowered the bucket into the well; a brisk yank on the rope tilted the bucket, allowing the water to flow in. When full, the hand-turned winch drew the full bucket to the surface. We had never seen anything like it.

Dad returned with an armload of dry wood. "Fuel won't be any problem, Susan," he cheered Mother. "Now, I'll see what can be done about getting the garden plowed. It's time to be planting peas and onions. While I'm gone, boys, bring in the rest of the wood I worked up."

"Ralph . . ." Mother began hesitantly. She ceased rummaging in the grocery box to look intently at her husband. John and I watched, puzzled. Something bothered Mother. What could it be?

"Susan," Dad reasoned, "we'll have to get the garden plowed. If we do it at once, we ought to have a good crop of vegetables."

"Who will you get to do it?" Mother asked resignedly. She carefully laid a fire in the stove and struck a match. The flame sputtered and died.

"Give it some air," counselled Dad, shifting the wood to allow for more circulation. "I'm going over to Smith's; they have a horse and plow. Maybe he can plow the garden for us." Mother sighed.

Dad vanished through the trees. By the time he returned two hours later, the house had been put in order and dinner was waiting. An unshaven, slovenly man driving a bony work horse accompanied Dad. Behind the horse clanked a single-shovel plow.

"Whoa thar, you brute!" Mr. Smith roared, yanking heavily

on the reins. "Whoa, I said!" He clumsily looped the leather lines around the porch railing. "Where's that thar stove, Eagle?" Smith swore thickly. He stumbled up the steps and across the porch.

Mother gaped. John, Nancy, and I crouched fearfully behind the kitchen table. Mr. Smith was drunk! And his language! Vague memories of Apricot Alice stirred my mind. Apricot Alice had talked like Mr. Smith.

Awkwardly, Dad and our neighbor erected the Heatrola in the living room. Mother's eyes, puzzled and unhappy, watched the process uneasily. Her hand flew to her mouth as the stove tilted crazily. However, it righted itself and settled safely to the floor. With much fumbling, the pipe was fitted and that was over. Mother heaved a sigh of relief.

Dad followed Mr. Smith to the garden, but came back to the house a short time later for lunch. We children noticed a strange glint in his eyes; a strong unusual odor reached us across the table.

Silently, with wilted spirit, Mother served the meal.

"Now, Susan; don't be angry just because I took a drink with Smith," Dad admonished, spreading oleo on a slice of bread. "You know I'm not a drinking man, but we have to be neighborly with these people."

Mother said, "Oh, Ralph!"

"Well," Dad replied defensively, "we've got to be neighborly, don't we?"

"Yes, but . . ." Mother began, laying aside her fork.

"All right!" Dad interrupted angrily. "If one of them offers me a free drink, what harm is there if I accept it? I know when to quit, don't I?" Dad glared belligerently at Mother.

"It would be better not to start, Dad," Mother reasoned gently. "Then there'd be no need to stop."

We listened incredibly. This was our father, speaking like this to our mother? Surely they sometimes disagreed, but never before had we heard Dad address Mother as he had now. Did Dad drink back in the old home? Mother must have known, but John and I couldn't answer that question positively.

The miserable uncertainties of that first day faded into the background as we worked together planting the garden and trimming the lawn. Dad nailed the clapboards in place and cut more wood. The neighbors, who really weren't too near, kept to themselves.

"I must find work of some sort, Susan," Dad remarked as he stored the garden tools in the basement. "We can't raise flour, or yeast, or soap, or kerosene for the lamps."

"I've yeast started, Ralph," Mother replied eagerly. She moved quickly up the stairs to the kitchen. "See." The fermented mixture smelled sour to me, but if Mother said it would make bread, I believed her.

"As for soap," Mother continued, "I can make my own with all the wood ashes and meat scraps. I've seen Grandmother do it often." She paused significantly. "The days are longer now. We won't need the lamps."

"Don't you *want* me to find work, Susan?" Dad snapped irritably. He slapped a chunk of wood viciously into the cook stove, jarring the teakettle.

"I suppose you must, Ralph," Mother acknowledged, "but— but—but, I'm afraid." Tears seeped from her eyes.

Dad softened. "Mother, please don't fret. Smith needs help. He'll pay me well and I promise I won't touch the stuff. I never did like it, you know. Okay?"

Mother couldn't reply. Dad stomped from the house. That day he became a helper with neighbor Smith in his illegal whiskey operation.

III

FARTHER AND FARTHER FROM GOD

Dad returned from the Smith place on Tuesday toting a square cardboard box. We watched curiously as he smilingly deposited it on the table before Mother.

"Susan, this ought to make you happy," he cajoled, patting her on the shoulder. Mother shook her shoulder roughly, dislodging Dad's hand. Evidently his peace offering would not be accepted, sight unseen.

Gingerly, Mother lifted one corner of the lid. That action produced an excited cackle from the setting hen inside the carton. Mother leaned over for a better look.

Dad threw back the top of the box. "She isn't wild, Susan. Biddy was a pet of the family. Smith's old woman sent some eggs, too." He placed his hand under the large black hen, withdrawing a handful of velvety brown eggs. "You can pay her back when you begin to get eggs," Dad added happily. "Put her in the chicken house, Ken, and feed her the table scraps."

Although Mother smiled at us when we gathered Biddy's box into our arms to take her to the hen house, her eyes were sad. When we walked past Dad as he washed up for supper, we caught a whiff of the same odor which pervaded our home the day Mr. Smith plowed the garden. Was Dad drinking again? Was that why Mother looked so unhappy?

Our startled faces must have drawn Dad's attention. His eyes flashed angrily. A curse ripped from his lips. We fled to the chicken house. We stayed there, talking to Biddy and making her comfortable, until Mother called us for supper. By that time Dad's anger was gone.

Following the meal John and I brought our school books to the table. We forgot Dad and his moods as we pursued our lessons. Nancy crawled on a chair beside me and plagued us with questions. I was struggling with a page of map study exercises.

"What are those squiggly blue things?" she asked, pointing to the large lake area of northern Canada.

"Those are lakes, silly," I replied.

John paused in his tussle with mathematics to glance at the map in my geography book. "There must be millions of them," he observed in an awed tone.

That map fascinated me. Lakes riddled the northern section of Canada, but I found very few black dots, indicating towns. Did people live here? What was this country like? If folks did live in this lake country, how did they make a living? Wouldn't it be cold, this far north? John broke into my thoughts.

"Here's a lake named Knee Lake," he grinned, "and a Bear Lake, and even a Cold Lake." He mused, "I wonder how they get their names."

"Here's one called—" I paused considering carefully— "Ath-a-bas-ca," I managed, "and another named Primrose." I scanned the map eagerly. "Here in Alberta is one named Calling Lake." I stopped, confused. I didn't understand it; those names possessed strange power. They haunted me, seeming to call me, urging me to come. John appeared not to notice my distraction.

"This one is Southern Indian Lake," John informed me, pointing to a sprawling body of water in Manitoba. Indian? Was northern Canada Indian country? Probably I would never know.

Mother ended our impromptu map lesson. "Hurry, boys, with your lessons. We don't have extra kerosene for the lamp." Baby Vernon fretted as Mother sat near the stove and rocked him. Dad stood glumly at the north window in the living room. He shifted his position and covertly studied Mother, still absently rocking Vernon. Abruptly, he stomped into the kitchen.

"Susan," he stormed, "now don't you say one word! I'm tired of just working for Smith. I'm going into partnership with him. Instead of wages, I'll share the profits, and believe me, they're good."

Mother's rocking halted. Her face blanched and her eyes filled with tears.

"Oh, no, Ralph! We can get along . . ." she protested weakly.

"Shut up, I tell you!" Dad shouted, slamming the screen door. From the porch he turned to glare at Mother, but she had buried her face in her apron and was weeping uncontrollably. John and I dared ask no questions. Dad marched defiantly into the woods. Was he going back to the Smith place? If so, why?

Mother had supper on the table when Dad's heavy footsteps sounded on the inside basement stairs. His mood had changed and he jovially took his place at the table.

"Just think of it, Susan!" he exulted. "Smith and I can turn out twice his volume and half the profits will be ours. We can soon have new shoes for the boys, and good trousers. You can get a new dress—anything you want," Dad said magnanimously.

"Ralph," Mother said with a hard glint in her eyes, and steel in her voice, "I'd rather go barefoot and with patches upon patches than to earn my clothing by making liquor. And don't you forget it!" Startled, I glanced at John from the corner of my eye. His mouth gaped, too. The voice that had spoken hardly sounded like that of our gentle, sweet-tempered mother.

Dad attacked from another direction. He turned to John and me. "You boys want good clothes and shoes, don't you?" he coaxed. We looked at our overalls, literally, as Mother had said, with patches upon patches. We pondered our shoes with the torn welts and ripped soles. If this venture of Dad's worked out as he hoped it would . . .

Tight lipped, Mother asked, "Where would you sell the stuff?"

Assuming by her question that Mother's opposition was lessening, Dad replied quickly, "Oh, Smith has already taken care of that. The hotel in Oberlin will buy most of the extra volume we produce. Cousin Cass . . ."

Mother cut him off shortly. "The hotel? In Oberlin? What are you talking about, Ralph?" Mother stared steadily at Dad, waiting for an answer.

Slowly, Dad's face flushed. Color crept down his neck, under the collar of his soiled shirt. "Well, it—it—it isn't a hotel, exactly. But everyone calls it that," Dad stammered. "And the sign on the front says 'Hotel Oberlin.' "

Mother carefully cut her meat. Slowly, she lifted a piece on the fork in her hand. Fearfully, she asked, "If it isn't a hotel, Dad, what is it? There isn't any need for a rooming house out here in the hills, is there?"

Dad shuffled his feet and hitched his chair forward. He growled at Mother, replying, "All right! So it's a brothel! They're going to get their liquor somewhere. Why shouldn't it be from us? Their money is just as good as anyone else's, isn't it? It'll buy shoes and dresses and flour, won't it?"

"Oh, Ralph!" Mother said, almost too stunned to speak. "If you must make the stuff, can't you sell it somewhere else? We can't have anything to do with a place like that."

"Shut up, woman! This is my business, and I'll run it as I please," Dad snapped. "And while we're on the subject," Dad added, "I've set a beer barrel in the basement. Keep your hands off!" Mother's lips set in a thin hard line. She said nothing.

Apparently Dad's business venture caused Mother to realize how helpless she really was. She came to John and me on Sunday morning while Dad slept off an excess of Mr. Smith's generosity, and said, "Boys, I want you to take Nancy and go to church today. It isn't right that we live like this, and God isn't pleased. Will you go?" She sighed, surveying her own figure now large with child and added, "If only I could walk that far, I'd go with you." Reluctantly we agreed to go.

Mother smiled. The sadness left her face and she looked almost happy again. If our going to church brought such results, of course we would go.

The church stood near the little one-room school about a mile and a half from our shack. Most of those attending were farmers who lived on the fringe of the hill area. Very few "hillbillies" ever went to church.

We created quite a stir. "Look, Mama! no socks!" one little girl squealed in a loud whisper, as we walked toward the door after the service ended. "And you can see his toes through the hole in his shoe," she added. The wearer of those shoes happened to be John.

I came in for a different type of ridicule. "Hello, Patches!" a boy about my age sneered. "Say, Paul," he chuckled to a friend, "did you ever see a patched patch? Here is one."

My hand doubled into a sturdy fist as I prepared to put that youth in his place. John snared my arm before I could deliver the punch and said, "Let's get out of here."

"If that's the way people act who go to church, I don't want to go," John declared to Mother upon our return.

"Not all churches are that way," Mother replied desperately. "Don't you remember our church at home, John? The people there were kind and friendly and gentle. They wouldn't have made fun of you."

"These sure did, and I'm not going back," I announced to Mother, "no matter what you say." Mother's cheeks paled. I had never spoken harshly to her before and I was immediately sorry, but I was also too proud and too stubborn to say so.

Unknown to us however, in response to Mother's prayers back in the old home, events were taking shape which would completely alter our lives.

IV

STRANGE ARRIVAL

Dad's business arrangements with Mr. Smith became a reality. Curiosity and fear of Dad's wrath caused John and me to co-operate with him in his beer-brewing operation in the basement of our home. Mother begged us not to become involved with the beer kegs. We assured her we could work with them without drinking the product. The smell, we declared, was enough for us.

"Here you are, boys," Dad announced thickly sometime after beginning his project. "Try this." He extended a bottle of clear, sparkling amber to John, who drew back hesitantly.

"Ralph! No!" Mother protested frantically. She sprang from the rocker, placing baby Ellen in her crib. Snatching Dad's arm, she cried, "Ralph Eagle, you must not teach these boys to drink!"

Dad swore savagely. He pushed Mother aside. "Shut up, woman! I'm running this place. I want the boys to taste this beer." He grinned crookedly at us. "Come on, boys. Be men! Taste it."

"No, boys!" Mother pleaded, her face pale and haggard. "Please don't touch it."

Dad cursed Mother, telling her again to "shut up." "One little taste won't hurt you," he insisted to John and me. I don't know why, but we took that fatal first sip.

Mother sobbed. We couldn't understand why. Just one swallow of beer wouldn't make us drunkards. Now I realize that Mother knew the pattern of alcoholism; we did not.

With the burden of caring for Baby Ellen in addition to her household chores, Mother became cross and fretful. Mother's opposition to Dad's work did not lessen, and when we boys began to liberally sample each new batch of "home brew," Mother's spirit sagged and almost failed.

"We must start back to church," Mother reminded us desperately the first Sunday in September, following our third year in the hills. "It isn't right that we live like this. God . . ."

"Yeah, I know," I hooted. " 'God isn't pleased.' Well, I don't care if He is or not. Do you, John?"

John laughed. "He'll have to show me He actually exists

before I'll worry about whether or not He's pleased with what I do."

"John!" Mother chided. "It's dangerous to talk that way. You must not." John laughed derisively.

One step down led to another. Before we recognized what had happened, we found ourselves cursing and damming Mother, Dad, and each other. Even Nancy picked up our foul language and used it as freely as we. Life wasn't very pleasant in those days. The happy days in the old home when Dad and Mother had worshipped the Lord together, seemed almost like a dream; the hymns of the little church we attended there faded to a very faint memory.

Mother didn't send Nancy to school when the fall term began. She needed her to help in caring for Ellen and Vernon. Nancy's nimble feet and deft fingers were useful in other ways as well.

"Here, Nancy, hang this on the line now," Mother instructed, handing Nancy one of her aprons. Mother stooped over the wash tub on the back porch, rinsing the hand-laundered clothing.

"But, Mom, it isn't clean," Nancy protested, displaying a soiled area on the front of the garment.

"I don't care. Hang it up," Mother snapped curtly.

Nancy flopped the apron over the line at a crazy angle. Mother noticed, but ignored Nancy's sloppy performance. She rinsed another garment and threw it to Nancy to be hung.

"This one is dirty, too, Mom," Nancy scolded.

"Hang it up, Nancy!" Mother ordered venomously. She ranted, "I'm through caring how things look around this place. No one else . . ." She caught herself before the oath slipped out and retreated. "No one else cares; why should I?" Mother's troubled glance followed John and me as we carried heavy buckets of water to the basement for Dad to reset the beer barrels. She had been forced to carry her own wash water from the rain barrel because neither of us "had time" to do it for her. Her unkempt appearance and hopeless eyes had ceased to trouble us.

Vernon tagged at my heels, whining like an injured puppy. At last I grasped him under the arms, prepared to administer a cure for his fussiness. The warmth of his body startled me. Even I realized that Vernon must be ill. I took him to Mother.

"Woman," I said, copying Dad's arrogant manner, "this brat is sick. Do something for him."

Mother dropped Dad's shirt into the tub and took Vernon into her arms. She felt his fevered head. Her glance swept our neglected yard. "Nancy, take care of Vernon while I hang these things. I'll gather some herbs for tea. Stir the fire so the water will be hot." Every hill garden offered a variety of plants designed to meet any emergency. Mother made tea from the "fever plant" and gave it to Vernon regularly throughout the day, but this fever stubbornly refused to subside. In spite of all her known home remedies, it didn't respond to treatment.

Eventually, the fever departed; not, however, without leaving us with a constant reminder of its visit. That illness had been polio. It resulted in mental retardation and a crippled hand for Vernon.

"Why did God allow this to happen to Vernon?" Mother cried one blustery Saturday morning in November.

John and I poked our noses from under the cook stove so we could hear the conversation. The fires had been reluctant to burn, and the house was cold, but we discovered a lovely warm spot under the stove.

"I doubt if God had anything to do with it," Dad growled, chewing on his ever-present cheroot. He jabbed the poker about in the stove, stirring the smoldering kindling.

"Oh, but He must have had," Mother declared, mixing flour and milk into our scanty supply of eggs to stretch them. "He must be saying something to us. Maybe He's telling us we've forgotten Him too long." She sighed heavily, running a hand through her prematurely white hair. "My mother used to say that He has some plan behind everything that happens. There has to be some purpose in this."

Dad slammed the poker into the woodbox. "Don't ask me about it, woman. You and your God will have to figure it out." Dad swore as the kitchen door jarred behind him. He stormed over the porch and down the steps.

Half-heartedly Mother washed the dishes and swept the floor. With dragging feet she spread a clean sheet on the table before the window and placed the hand irons on the stove to heat. Carelessly, she tossed flour, salt, and lard into a large dishpan and added liquid yeast and water. She kneaded the dough casually and set it on the back of the stove to rise.

Taking a hot iron from the stove, Mother turned to the table. A moving object in our lane riveted her attention. An automobile, completely strange to our part of the hills, worked its way meticulously around our boulders.

"Kenneth! John!" Mother called urgently. "Come here." We sensed the tension in her voice and bounced from the living room into the kitchen. "Do you know that car?"

A clean shiny blue Plymouth sedan with black fenders pulled up before the house.

"No," we replied. Revenuers? Could it be revenuers? They seldom bothered the hill people, but who else could it be? We watched while the driver parked outside our rickety fence. A young man, clean and shaven, neatly dressed, got out. He stood for a long time with his hand on our gate. At last he opened it and walked toward the house. Of one thing only we were positive—he didn't "belong" to the hills!

V

ENTER—BROTHER ALBERT

The young man rapped lightly on our door. Mother motioned for John to open it. Outside the doorway, hat in hand, stood our visitor.

Nothing in his appearance identified him with the hills. Noticeably missing were the tobacco stained whiskers, uncut hair, soiled clothing, and characteristic slouch of many of our hill citizens. And when he spoke, his voice seemed to echo back to another era.

"Good morning, Mrs. Eagle." The visitor bowed slightly and smiled. "I'm Albert Lightfoot. May I come in?"

Mother paused uncertainly between stove and table. "What's your business?" she demanded sourly.

"I'm a servant of the Lord, m'am, and I'm interested in your souls," Mr. Lightfoot responded. "May I come in and talk to you about it?"

"I reckon," Mother replied, rather grudgingly.

Mr. Lightfoot smiled at John and me and asked our names and ages. We replied grumpily and hastily squeezed into the corner of the kitchen nearest the basement door. That exit was our escape route should escape become advisable or necessary.

Ellen fretted in her crib and Mother sat down in the rocker with her. This gave our guest the opportunity he had been waiting for.

"Do you realize you have a double responsibility to your children, Mrs. Eagle?" he asked gently. John and I stared at the man. He spoke in riddles.

"I'm not sure what you're getting at, sir," Mother replied, responding to his friendly attitude.

Mr. Lightfoot indicated the ironed garments stacked on the kitchen table, the pot of beans boiling with a ham hock on the stove. "I see you have provided physically for your family. You also have a spiritual responsibility toward them." He reached for Ellen who surprised every one by cooing eagerly to be taken. He cuddled the baby expertly in his arms, continuing, "This dear little girl, Mrs. Eagle—this bundle of possibilities—could grow up to be one of the worst of criminals, or she can be a woman of God." He paused significantly, "Much of what type of person she becomes depends upon you."

Tears came to Mother's eyes. "I sent them to the church down at the schoolhouse, but people made fun of their patched clothing," Mother answered. "I didn't have the heart to send them back." Mr. Lightfoot shook his head sadly.

"We have a little mission in the hills in Oberlin," Mr. Lightfoot stated. "We meet in Jackson's store. We're all common people, so no one will laugh at you. We want you to come; will you?"

"That is too far to walk . . ." Mother began.

"My wife and I will come for you," Mr. Lightfoot said cheerfully. Vernon toddled into the room and stood looking intently at the visitor. The young man studied the tot covertly and said laconically to Mother, "Polio?"

"I reckon," Mother replied, weeping. "Why, Mr. Lightfoot? Why did God allow that to happen to Vernon? He was such a bright baby . . ."

"I'm not sure I have the answer, Mrs. Eagle. Perhaps He was trying to get your attention." He smiled quietly and prodded, "*Had* you forgotten Him?"

"Oh, yes!" Mother replied, sobbing audibly. The tears dropped into her splotched apron. "I don't see how anyone can even love us anymore—we've gotten that far away from God."

I thought I saw tears glistening in our guest's eyes as he answered, "That's the wonderful thing about our God, Mrs. Eagle. Even when we turn our backs on Him and go our own way, He still loves us. He still seeks us and even now He is seeking you." He stood up and looked into Ellen's dancing blue eyes. "I'll see you tomorrow morning then, little friend?" he asked, tweaking a pink ear, but listening for Mother's reaction to his question.

"Yes!" Mother said with a real smile. I couldn't recall when I had last seen her with a happy, cheerful expression. It did funny things to me.

"John? Kenneth?" he inquired.

I looked at Mother. I thought of Dad's operation with Smith and the beer keg in the basement. I wondered if our guest noticed the faint unique odor permeating the house. I meditated briefly upon the atmosphere of our home since Dad had gone into business with Smith. Those head-splitting hangovers raced through my mind as I remembered my own experimentation with liquor. Was it really worth it? I made a hasty decision.

"I'll go," I decided.

"I will, too," John echoed.

Nancy dashed in from the chicken house with two brown eggs. Mother duly introduced her to Mr. Lightfoot and in the end all five of us had agreed to attend Sunday school the next day.

The change that came over our home following this visit startled us. Mother hummed an old gospel song. The melody tugged at my memory; I struggled to recall the words. "In-fin-ite day . . ." and "never withering flowers" teased my mind, but I couldn't put the song together. I almost hoped the congregation would sing the hymn, so I could hear those long forgotten lines.

Mother rose bright and early Sunday morning. She hummed another old song as she prepared breakfast. The tenseness had left her face and the shadow of despair which had haunted her eyes for so long seemed fainter.

Dad noticed the change of morale in our home. He slouched in the doorway connecting the kitchen and living room, observing tartly, "You're getting pretty good, aren't you, going to church?" Sneeringly, he continued, "You're a lot better than other people. Soon you'll be too good to live with me." He stooped to peer into Mother's troubled eyes and accused, "Won't you?" Mother reined her anger and continued slipping Ellen's freshly ironed frock over her blond head.

The sudsy washcloth in my hand attracted Dad's attention. I wasn't fond of soap, and never used it if I could avoid it, so it shouldn't have shook me when Dad took note of my ablutions. His gaze raked my clean hands and the fringe of damp hair framing my face. "What are *you* going to be?" he scoffed. "One of Jesus' boys, too?" He puffed furiously on the stub of his cheroot. Brother Lightfoot's beautiful blue sedan edged around the boulders in our lane, and Dad vanished through the cellar door into the basement.

Sally Lightfoot won our affection immediately with her happy interest in us. She knew our names and ages. Under her gentle influence, our tongues loosened and we talked freely of school activities, and of Biddy and her family, but we studiously shied away from conversation that might involve Dad and his occupation.

It wasn't that Smith's still, and Dad's part in it, was a secret. The "right" people—those who patronized the industry—knew of it, but we couldn't be sure how widely our reputation had spread in other circles. However, in the genial warmth of this wholesome couple, our home activities assumed an ugly viciousness. It didn't occur to me on that bright November day that the path upon which I had entered led straight to the crossroads, where a life-or-death decision would be unavoidable.

VI

MISSION OBERLIN

At the end of our rocky, rutted lane the Lightfoot vehicle veered east toward Oberlin. Customarily, our three-mile trek to high school took us westward toward Milltown. The occasions when John and I visited Oberlin were rare.

True, we realized that Smith's primary "business" outlet existed in Oberlin, but he managed distribution. Therefore, we had hardly given the geography of the village a second thought on previous visits there.

Brother Lightfoot negotiated an acute right turn in the gravel road. He braked gently as the road sloped downward. It swerved around an ancient barn built of multicolored rocks. The car crept to a halt beside two other vehicles parked in front of Jackson's General Store.

Our eyes must have bulged when we stepped from the car and straightened to examine our surroundings. Facing us from directly across the road stood the Oberlin Hotel with its long front porch, two full-storied height, and many narrow windows. It was almost ten a.m. but the place appeared deserted.

The small congregation, mostly hill people like ourselves, welcomed us warmly. Never, since identifying ourselves with the outlaws, desperadoes, and outcasts of the hills, had we been received anywhere with such genuine love and enthusiasm.

At the door of the building a tall, slightly balding man waited to welcome us. From my vista of fifteen years, he was old, at least thirty. I know now that appearances can be deceitful; the life span of Allen Martz at that time covered twenty-five years.

Brother Lightfoot introduced us. "Brother Allen, I've brought two students for your class, John and Kenneth Eagle." He turned to John and me. "Your teacher, boys. Allen Martz."

Allen smiled broadly and shook our hands. He surveyed my gangly height and grinned boyishly. "Eagle, eh? Can you soar like one, Kenneth?"

Slightly flustered because I wasn't sure exactly what Allen Martz meant when he asked if I could "soar like an eagle," I failed to muster a speedy comeback. John found one. "No," he quipped, "but he can run like a deer when he's scared."

Allen laughed and replied, "Oh, when I'm frightened I can run like a deer, too." We liked him for placing himself on our level. We sensed an immediate bond of friendship with the big man.

It seems strange to us now, but that day neither Allen nor myself had any intuition of the unusual and marvelous ways the Lord would move in our lives. We had no inkling of a future meeting in the north many miles from Oberlin, or of winging our way together over barren areas of the northern wilderness lake country. But that belongs to another era of history.

Rows of folding chairs lined each side of the store. We took seats to the left of the building. Curiously I studied the rows and rows of drawers lining the walls. Each drawer front was perhaps four inches square and sported a neat pull knob. Below the rows of drawers were bins for flour and white and brown sugar. On the open shelves to the right, bolts of cotton and calico invited our attention. A sign above a large glass container placed on one shelf said in bold letters, "dried fruit." On the shelf above the fruit another sign identified an odd assortment of bottles as natural mineral oils.

"Let's turn to hymn number 153."

Startled, my consciousness jumped back to proceedings in the building. I noticed now the large printed poster behind the speaker's stand. "The Lord is in His holy temple; let all the earth keep silence before Him." In the brief interval before Allen Martz began leading the music, I puzzled the phenomenon of the admonition to keep silence before the Lord—and yet everyone seemed prepared to sing. Oh, well, what difference did it make?

We had never before collided with the Gospel as Allen Martz presented it in our Sunday school lesson, or as Abner Lightfoot, Albert's twin brother, preached it from the pulpit. John and I practiced an eye for an eye—or if you please, a fist blow for a fist blow—a harder one for your brother than he had given you, if you were man enough to accomplish it. But love your enemy, do good to them that hate you! Turn the other cheek when someone hits you! Not I! That would be cowardly, and, I assured myself, I was no coward. Nevertheless, this philosophy intrigued me. I mused on the possibilities of what further curious and unworkable notions Brother Allen might harbor. It might be interesting to find out.

"Do you like to hunt, Kenneth?" Allen Martz asked, following the service as we waited for the congregation to file from the building.

"Not much," I replied. "John is the hunter."

"Oh. What do you hunt mostly, John?" he asked.

John grinned at me. By the twinkle in his eyes, I realized

what was coming. "Well, we're having 'possum for dinner today," he announced.

His declaration didn't bring the reaction John had expected. Instead of saying, "Opossum! Surely you don't eat them!" Allen Martz said calmly, "I've never tasted one. I'd like to try it sometime."

"I'll get you one," John agreed.

"Your mother will have to tell Mrs. Martz how to fix it," the teacher warned.

"Oh, she'll be happy to," I replied. I looked for Mother. She was visiting with Betsy Martz, who sat with our Ellen cradled against her shoulder, sound asleep. Mother smiled at us and years seemed to vanish from her face.

Vernon left Mother to seek attention elsewhere. "When is your birthday?" he inquired, looking into Allen's face.

"July fourth. Can you remember that?" Allen returned genially.

"Oh, yes," Vernon answered.

"Good!" our new friend responded. John and I exchanged amused grins. Knowing as he must of Vernon's mental deficiency, Allen didn't expect Vernon to retain his birth date. He would learn.

Finally we reached the door. Abner Lightfoot gave each of us a small paper. Casually glancing at the contents, I discovered a character who drank. This aroused my interest. Before we arrived home I had read the entire section. It ended with the words, "To be continued."

Amazingly, living conditions described in that brief chapter of *Lucy Winchester* paralleled our own in many ways. It set me thinking. Did the family lick the problem? If so, how? To my own surprise, I wanted to know.

Allen Martz and Betsy had driven us home. "We'll see you next Sunday?" He asked cheerfully when we arrived at our front door.

"Yes!" Mother said emphatically.

He looked questioningly to John and me. "Yes," we nodded.

Some of the cheer remained, even in our dreary, squalid home. I found myself joining Mother as she hummed, "There's a city of light 'mid the stars we are told . . ." The tenor rang through my memory like the chime of bells. I couldn't erase it.

Dad didn't enjoy the music. The changed atmosphere in the home annoyed him. At last he exploded, "Will you shut up? I've got a headache!" Even that angry outburst failed to silence us completely, much to his chagrin.

VII

DOWN DECISION ROAD

Lucy Winchester captivated our family. So many of our household problems were similar; for example, the shortage of food. Poor Clem must have his alcohol: Dad's greatest necessity (he already had the alcohol, our "Eagle" brand of home brew) was his tobacco. That took precedence over everything else, including food.

In one installment of the story, Lucy sent her children to ask the neighbors for potato peelings so the family would have something to eat. We didn't need to do that, but in the spring when we could no longer eat wild game, and the meat was all gone, food became very scarce. Necessity compelled Mother to improvise to feed us. She gathered, cooked and seasoned wild greens, and mixed them with bread crumbs, thus stretching the available food so it would be enough to serve the family. Although we grumbled at the unsightly "goop," the dish tasted delicious.

In other ways, we identified with Lucy. Mother's resistance to alcohol and its influence in our home; her sense of obligation to God—these reminded us uncomfortably of Mother, yet it gave the story great appeal. We discussed each new chapter constantly, at the table and around the living room fire in the evening.

We saved those papers every Sunday and stacked them neatly on the rickety living room what-not.

"Ken, these papers are all out of order," John scolded one Sunday when he placed the latest edition on the stack.

"I haven't touched them," I replied grumpily.

John rearranged the papers, placing the current paper on the bottom of the pile. We forgot the subject as both of us settled down at the kitchen table to catch up on our home work. Since John was now a senior and I a junior in high school, our work load had increased tremendously. We usually spent most of Sunday afternoon sweating over our books.

Once, I noticed unconcernedly, Dad clomped into the living room and a few minutes later, walked back out. Shortly after that, Nancy plopped the dishpan onto its nail and dashed into the living room.

"John, why didn't you put the *YCC* where it belongs?" she called querulously. "I haven't read it yet."

"It's right on the bottom of the stack where it's supposed to be," John retorted.

"It isn't," Nancy snapped. "I've looked through the whole lot and it isn't here. Ken, did you have it?"

"No," I replied.

"Well, where is it then?" Nancy demanded testily, coming to the door to glare stormily at the two of us.

John pushed aside his book and marched into the living room. He returned with a bewildered frown. "It isn't there, Ken. You and I weren't in there. Mother and the kids are asleep. The only person who was in there was—Say! Do you think Dad might have taken it to read?" he asked.

We stared at each other incredulously.

"It's possible," Nancy remarked at last. "He's heard us talk so much about it, he might have gotten curious."

"And he was in there a little while ago," I added.

"Let's let it go and not say anything about it," John suggested. "Wait until later, Nancy, and see if it gets back on the stack. Then we'll know for sure if Dad took it to read."

In the hub-bub of evening chores, supper, and dishes, we forgot the paper. When it did occur to Nancy again, the missing issue was lying on top of the pile. We were delighted. Nancy could hardly wait for an opportunity to whisper the astonishing news to Mother.

The atmosphere in our home improved as we continued to attend the services at the mission. However, our hearts were unchanged; we were still unsaved. Dad remained a bootlegger. We continued to quarrel and fight among ourselves. Our tempers flared at the most trivial incidents. This attitude carried over into school life, where it sometimes brought drastic results.

To attend high school, John and I walked the three miles between our shack and Milltown morning and evening. Weather conditions didn't change that fact. We walked in the cold, wind, snow, and driving sleet. We walked, often with shoes that were coming apart at the seams or that needed soles. We attended school, although, as Mother sighed, we were growing like weeds, and our wrists and ankles seemed to shoot from our flimsy clothing. Of course we got cold; the biting winds of winter whistled about our ears and penetrated our worn coats. Nevertheless, we determined to be prepared for a better vocation than the one we were presently engaged in, so we plodded six miles a day to and from high school.

But, to return to school problems.

I don't recall now exactly how it happened. Probably I insulted tall, burly Lewis Jones with my big mouth and he, in rebuttal, did the unforgiveable. He referred slightingly to my family background.

"You needn't think you're so great," Lewis sneered at me. "You're just a hillbilly—bootlegger Ralph's brat."

"Leave my family out of this!" I shot back. I was too angry to think clearly. I challenged, "This is between the two of us. Do you want to settle it with a fair fight?"

The bell jingled. Lewis agreed crisply, "Sure. In the gym, at noon." At that time "fair," or supervised, fights were allowed in the gymnasium.

I nodded to my friends who were standing about, "Come and watch." The invitation really wasn't necessary; wild horses couldn't have kept them away.

So cocky and arrogant was I, and so certain of victory, that I hardly gave the contest a second thought. John had never been able to best me, so why worry about Lewis? Oh, sure, Lewis topped the scales with a few more pounds than John did, but that was a minor thing. It really wouldn't matter when the chips were down.

At noon, the sliding doors to the gym were pushed aside. Lewis and I sparred lightly, each looking for a punch which could be used to advantage against the other. I seized an opening and knocked him to the floor. I was on top.

"Ha, ha! I've got him now!" I thought jubilantly.

Little did I realize that Lewis was playing cat and mouse with me. With one mighty flip of his muscular arms he rolled me over. I was on the bottom now, and he was on top. Lewis weighed over two hundred pounds, and I not nearly that much. Too late, I recognized the advantage those extra pounds gave him. To my dismay I found that I was helpless!

I would have screamed and cried if I could have, but Lewis finished my resistance too effectively and efficiently to allow for words or pleas of any kind. He stood up and the spectators lifted his hands high, proclaiming, "The winner!" I had to be helped from the floor. As I almost crept to the locker room, everyone standing by jeered, "Bo-o-o, Eagle!" That crushing defeat thoroughly deflated my ego. My friends had come to watch me win, not lose!

"Fighting never settles anything," Mother sighed when she saw my condition that Friday evening. "I don't know why the school authorities allow it."

"If only I could have gotten in one good punch after I had him down; I'd have taught him a thing or two . . ." I began belligerently.

"No, Kenneth," Mother reasoned, "it wouldn't be any different if you had won. Our trouble is inside of us—the wickedness in our hearts. That's what caused you to fight with Lewis to begin with, isn't it?"

Her words burned like fire. "When did you become a preacher?" I sneered, and slammed the basement door behind me. Right then I felt like "tying one on" but common sense warned me that getting drunk wouldn't solve the problem either. That would just obliterate it briefly. I sulked in the basement for awhile, then returned to the kitchen.

The thought of church on Sunday pulled me in opposite directions. One part of me longed to go and find freedom in Christ. The other part, the old man, resisted the voice of the Spirit. He counselled, "Everyone will know of the fight, and the fool you made of yourself. Don't go." After a soul-searching struggle, I decided to go.

We received the surprise of our existence that Sunday. Following breakfast, Dad casually washed and shaved. Although this was extremely out of character for him, no one commented about it, or questioned him concerning it. But when he joined us in the kitchen wearing his only suit, our curiosity became explosive; it must have stuck out of our ears.

"Well," Dad roared, as we started, "can't I go along to church without you all looking as if the sky had dropped?"

VIII

CROSSROADS

What a happy day for us! Dad—washed, shaved, dressed, and announcing his intention of going to Sunday school! I'm sure Allen and Betsy Martz were just as startled and as delighted as we, when they came by for us that winter morning.

In spite of Dad's decision to go to church, not everything was roses and cream. How can a home be happy when the individuals composing it are wretched and miserable? Satan controlled us; we floundered helplessly, trying to "do better." And even until now, I have yet to see a home controlled by Satan where there is real joy and happiness.

Summer came and went. John graduated from high school and found work in Philadelphia. When school began in September, I enrolled as a senior at Milltown High School. Now my homework tripled.

Miss Lantz, the teacher of the local one-room elementary school, encouraged Mother to send Vernon to school. As Allen Martz had found to his amusement, Vernon's memory in some things was phenomenal, especially in recalling birthdates.

"I'd like to try," Miss Lantz told Mother as they visited in our kitchen while Mother kneaded bread dough. "I believe he can learn to read. You'll send him with Nancy, won't you?"

"Yes," Mother nodded, tears glistening in her eyes. "I'll send him. It will be wonderful if he can be taught to read." She glanced out of the window where Vernon crossed the yard from the woodlot with an armload of kindling, and continued, "I'll miss him, though. He's such a help here; he carries in wood and water for me and amuses Ellen. I don't know what I'll do without him."

"But, if he can learn . . ." Miss Lantz said.

"Yes, yes, I know," Mother nodded quietly. "I'll send him to you."

Vernon's limited mental capacity responded to Miss Lantz's gentle teaching. He did learn to read. But arithmetic proved beyond his powers of comprehension and his crippled hand discouraged writing. However, he mastered the manipulation of larger tools, such as a hammer, with his left hand. A pencil was just too small, or else a few meaningless squiggles on paper didn't appear worth the effort to him. With a hammer or saw or axe, Vernon could see that something had been accomplished. Those tools were different.

Vernon came to love reading. He would read for hours to anyone who would listen, although I'm not sure how much he understood. This boomeranged into a real blessing for Mother. Ellen enjoyed being the sole object of Vernon's attention; she happily sat quietly while Vernon read for her.

October of that year I'll never forget. On Sunday, October 14, Brother Allen drove the family to the mission. Leaves of all hues fluttered to the ground as the car meandered over the narrow road, up and down the hills and around the boulders. I saw nothing of beauty in their demise, only death and darkness, a foreshadowing of the cold and bleakness of winter. Those bare, black branches reflected the bloom of my sin-shackled soul.

"Revivals begin tonight," Brother Abner Lightfoot announced at the close of the service that brilliant morning. "We urge all of you to come, especially if you need to get right with the Lord."

"You *will* come, won't you, Kenneth?" His eyes probed mine as he shook my hand at the door of the store building.

I couldn't look into the face of this compassionate man of God. I knew I was a sinner. I knew that Christ loved me. He had demonstrated that love through Albert Lightfoot, who had loved us when no one else did. But I also realized that if I attended those meetings I would be forced to make a decision about Christ. I wasn't ready to do that—not yet. I wretchedly studied the toes of my old shoes.

"You'll come, Kenneth?" he questioned again, hopefully.

"Maybe," I replied, not promising, and leaving a loophole through which I could squirm if I wished. I battled the issue all afternoon. When evening came, my course of action was still undetermined.

Everyone else in the family decided to attend the service that night. The enemy presented me with an acceptable variety of reasons why I should not. First: I didn't have my homework quite done; I'd have to work like mad to finish it in time. Second: I needed my rest; that six-mile walk plus a big day of study went better if a man had his full night's sleep. Third: With the other members of the family going, the car would be full enough without me. The list Satan conjured up was endless. He won the battle, temporarily. I wasn't going. Not tonight, anyway.

Although I was unaware of it at the time, two men of God

must have been praying mightily to Him in my behalf. Dad came in from the barn as I attempted to solve an algebra problem. Immediately things began to happen. They altered the course of my life.

Accusations flew. "Why didn't you feed the chickens this morning, like you were supposed to?" Dad demanded curtly.

His manner irritated me. My nerves stood on edge, due to the inner operation of the Holy Spirit, and my temper flared. I made no effort to subdue it.

"For your information, Dad, I did feed them and watered them, too," I shouted.

"You didn't," he shot back.

"I did," I replied angrily.

"If you fed them, why are they out of feed now?" Dad asked, his eyes flashing dangerously.

Anger beyond all reason gripped me. I swore savagely and told Dad I didn't know, but that I *had* fed his old chickens!

A gentle rap on the door brought us to our senses. The mission workers—Brother Allen probably! In our stormy argument we had failed to hear their approach. Had they heard me curse Dad to his face? What did Brother Allen think if he had? What could I do? I had to do something quickly to save face. Only one thing came to my mind. I did it.

"Oh, yes, Dad," I said loudly, so the individual outside the closed door would be sure to catch it, "Of course I'll go with you to the meeting."

Nothing in Allen Martz's manner betrayed him, if he had overheard our spat. I was positive, though, as the meeting progressed, that someone had tipped off the preacher. His message described precisely the scene which had taken place in our home that evening. Now, after walking with the Lord for many years, I understand how the Holy Spirit revealed our need to the evangelist, but that night I knew nothing of the miraculous power of that indwelling Spirit. I attributed the speaker's knowledge to a "tattletale."

The minister proceeded to speak of the two ways—the narrow way that leads to life; the broad way which leads to death. He enlarged upon uncertain "joys" and "pleasures" experienced by those journeying upon the broad road. "But," he emphasized, "those pleasures are brief. They are hollow and leave you with a vicious hangover." How true! I found myself mentally agreeing.

Neither did he minimize the hardship to be expected in the narrow way. "The Christian life is hard—very hard. In fact, your problems may just begin when you accept Christ as your

Saviour. But the joy of knowing Him, of finding your load of sin removed, of experiencing His forgiveness . . ." the speaker's eyes gleamed with an inner light; his voice trembled with emotion. He paused, dug into his pocket for a handkerchief, wiped his eyes, and continued, "Friends, nothing can equal the thrill of walking with God. Won't you accept Christ as Lord and Saviour, tonight?"

The congregation sang *Softly and Tenderly.* I wanted to come. Oh, how I longed to be free of that load of guilt and shame! But it seemed the Devil had some type of special glue that held me to my seat.

The first verse of the hymn ended, the second, and the third. Around me, a few people rose and walked forward. I yearned to come, but Satan hindered me. I cannot explain—it must have been because of the prayers of the saints—but as the last strains of the last chorus echoed sweetly in the old store building, with tears streaming down my face, I arose triumphantly and walked down the aisle to the altar.

IX

ALL THINGS NEW

Words can't describe it. Only those who have experienced it know what Paul means when he declares, "Behold, all things are become new."

I arose from my knees at Oberlin mission on October 14, a new man in Christ. Old things had indeed passed away—slipped off, been shed, laid aside—as a filthy garment. Everything became new. It is an experience that thrills me even today, when I recall that glorious night.

My first act as a child of God was a necessary, but humbling apology to Dad. That quarrel now stood between me and my God and marred my fellowship with Him. I found that unbearable.

"Da-a-d," I stammered, when we were arranged in Brother Allen's car for the trip home, "I'm sorry about the way I talked to you this evening. Will you forgive me?"

I hadn't realized silence could be heard. After a long minute, Dad cleared his throat; he shuffled his feet. Finally, he mumbled, "Sure, boy; forget it."

"Kenneth," Allen approved, "you're making a good beginning in your Christian life. These things *must* be taken care of when the Spirit brings them to our attention. If we don't, we lose our fellowship with God," he negotiated a bend around a boulder, "and nothing we could gain in this world would replace a loss such as that."

He was right. The load I had carried for the brief time after the Spirit caused me to understand that I must apologize to Dad, until I had opportunity to do so, convinced me. I determined that I would allow nothing to stand between me and my Saviour.

That problem disposed of, I gave my newly discovered senses over to reveling in the glory of the night. Had the stars ever been so near or so bright before? Did the moon always seem so friendly and immense? Those cottony white clouds drifting over the sky—had they never been there before? Or had I failed to notice them? And the mottled shadows on the road. Did moonlight against the trees always produce such intricate patterns? I concluded that, surely, these wonders existed before tonight, but my soul's eyes had needed cleansing in order to see them. My heart sang praises to God for the beauty of that night.

When we alighted from Brother Allen's car, the moment was too sacred to share. "I'll be in later, Dad," I said.

The family watched, curiously, I suspect, as I turned toward the Thousand Acre Forest back of our house. Many times I had badgered John or Vernon into accompanying me outdoors after dark because I was afraid. I figured that with the populace in our area, and with the nature of our vocation, someone might have a grudge against one of us. Someone just might be waiting in the dark with a gun to kill us. The murder mystery stories I loved to read didn't help the situation any, either. Anyway, I knew I wasn't ready to die and to bolster my courage, I insisted that John or Vernon go outside with me when this was necessary. It seems exceedingly silly now, but those were the facts!

Oh, the joy of freedom from fear! I walked on and on and on, into the very heart of the woodland. There I dropped to my knees before my God. Fear was forever banished from my heart that night. I felt the very presence of God. Sometimes since, in the northland with the wolves lifting their noses to the sky and howling, I've sensed that same personal Presence with me.

I now had discovered for myself what the evangelist meant when he said, "Nothing can equal the thrill of walking with God." Mutely, I mused as I reluctantly turned toward home. Beginning that journey with Him has been so sweet, so joyous. What will it be when I get to know Him better?

We continued to attend the Oberlin mission. The class period and preaching service assumed a vital place in my life. They supplied food for my soul. On November 18 I was baptized into the body of Christ, in that same old store building. It still stands today, a precious memento of God's grace and love.

The following Sunday, November 24, Mother cast her lot with the people of God, and shortly afterward, Dad joined us. However, John still was unwilling to yield his heart to the Lord.

The change that took place in our home defies description. The beer-making equipment, like the idols of ancient Israel, was stomped to pieces. Anything that wouldn't burn was broken to bits and carted away. Miraculously the cleansing of our souls brought rejuvenation to our physical surroundings. The joy of Lord in her heart gave Mother the incentive to brighten up the house. She washed windows and hung curtains. Geraniums—a gift of Betsy Martz—appeared at the windows. Dad cleared the yard of plunder and mended the fences. He did many odd jobs that, due to his former interests, had been neglected for years.

However, a new problem arose. Dad now lacked work. No bootlegging—no money. It was as simple as that!

The solution also proved simple. A "new" thing since Dad's conversion was family worship. Around the family circle in the evening, we claimed Christ's promise, "Ask and ye shall receive." We turned to God in faith and soon Dad found employment with a nearby farmer. Strange, before our conversion we hardly realized that farmers existed so near to us.

Nancy was fast growing into adolescence. Mother expressed a deep concern for her and for John, who scoffed at our "religion."

"Nancy is so stubborn, Kenneth," Mother worried. "She gets so angry if I correct her. What can I do?" Mother wrung her hands in distress, and continued, "And if I mention Christ, or her need of salvation to her . . ."

"Pray, Mother dear," I replied, adding encouragingly, "Read James 1:5. Ask God for wisdom to handle Nancy. He'll supply it. I'll be praying, too."

Mother smiled. Her eyes were tired. The years of sinful living had left their mark, but the joy of the Lord erased many of those lines. "You're such a comfort, Kenneth," she said. "I'm sure the Lord has a special place for you."

Those days were like the years in the backside of the desert for Moses, and Paul's stay in Arabia. I soaked up the Word of God; studied it, read it, and prayed over it. We discussed it together around the family altar. It became a precious Book, a Familiar Friend.

The atmosphere of our home changed in another way. One day Dad returned from an old-fashioned country auction with the news that he had bought an old family Bible. Mother had always wanted one; she said the large old book, lying open on the mantel, would quickly identify us as a God-fearing family to those who entered our home. However, due to their cost, her hopes of owning one had been slim.

"The auctioneer knocked it off on the first bid—a dollar and a half!" Dad ejaculated. "It's a beauty, isn't it?"

I fell in love with the old Book at first sight. The covers were embossed, of a soft, sooty black with gold lettering. As I examined the cover, I found a v-shaped wedge chipped in the top cover, evidently the work of some lad with a pocket knife. Somehow, that made the Book uniquely dear to me. I loved it and cherished it, even if its former owner had not!

Mother cried as she examined it. She sat down immediately and read Psalm 91, one of her favorites, for us, before placing the big volume reverently on the mantel. Somehow, the old Book seemed to blend right in with our dilapidated furniture— the massive old armchair bolstered by a six-inch block of wood where a leg was missing, the potbellied stove, the worn linoleum. Even the rainbow-hued, braided rugs, which covered the spots that had suffered most from the passage of many feet, ceased to seem out of place.

That old Bible lent a wonderful glow to our shabby dwelling. Mother soon discovered that its large print was much easier to read than her personal Bible. When she sat down to read for us at bed time, it seemed like the faded lilacs and roses on the wall paper smiled once more and became remarkably bright again.

I'll concede, Mother was no orator or polished reader. But God seemed so near when Mother read that old Bible. Many times as Mother read those familiar stories of Daniel and David, and daylight faded into darkness, the gloom would suddenly vanish. Then, as Mother sang softly, as she went about tidying up the house, we would sense a Heavenly Presence, right in our room under the eaves before we fell asleep.

How we praised the Lord for that old family Bible!

Although the Bible boosted our morale, it did not remove the problems of everyday living which plagued us daily.

Sometimes I wondered why God, in His omnipotence, had chosen to place us among the outcasts and criminals of the hills. Why had He put us here? Why did He not leave us in our old home nearer the city? Gradually I began to see a small portion of His plan. He seemed to be telling me, "I have children who are willing to seek my lost sheep if they can enjoy the comfort and ease of the city. So few are willing to work here, among the lost sheep of these hills. This is where I need you."

Here, among these rugged individuals, God was conditioning me to work among uncultured people—the rejects of modern society. I didn't know yet what form of service it would be. I only knew that He was calling—calling—calling. At times, in desperation, I went out to the barn and threw myself face down in the hay. "Lord, I know you're calling me. What do you want me to do?" I could discern no answer to that cry.

In looking back, if it hadn't been for those years among the outcasts and desperadoes, life wouldn't be for me what it is today. Perhaps, had we not moved into these hills, no one would have cared for our souls—as David expressed it. I thank God from the bottom of my heart for those years in "Hill School."

X

CHRIST—A REALITY

That six mile trek to and from school now became an exploration of discovery. Frost glittering on the wire fences, clinging to each blade of grass and sparkling in the chilling light of early morning; cloud patterns of each new day—now angry and dark—now soft and fluffy, as the mood of the day dictated. The sounds around me—chipmunks scampering into their holes under a root, squirrels chattering and quarreling in the tree tops; the clacking call of the blue jay—these all impressed themselves indelibly upon my joyously receptive senses. I marvelled that so many wonderful things had always existed, but the same pair of physical eyes which were seeing them now had failed to comprehend them in the past. How I praised the Lord for spiritual eyesight!

"The annuals are here, Eagle," Joel Adams announced when I entered home room one February morning.

"Oh?" I replied casually.

"Yes," he replied grinning. I felt my skin prickle. Joel was up to something. Several other seniors gathered around to enjoy the fun.

I didn't know what to say, so I said nothing, which—I've discovered—is usually a safe policy.

"Did you see the class prophecy?" he prodded, to my increasing bewilderment.

"No."

"What do you think they're predicting for you?" Joel teased.

"I've no idea," I replied. I decided that since Joel evidently had determined to see this through, I might as well play along and get it over with. "What are the 'prophets' predicting for me? I'm curious."

My interest surprised them but Joel recovered instantly. He flipped the book open and read clearly, "Kenneth Eagle will leave school to become a preacher." Everyone laughed uproariously but me.

"What do you think of that, Eagle?" Joel demanded through his laughter.

I considered. Me—bootlegger Ralph's son—a preacher? Not likely! Leave school? Not before graduating, if I could help it.

Seriously, I answered, "I've no intention of leaving school before graduation. As for the other part of the prediction—I am a Christian, but I don't ever expect to be a minister."

My sober reply killed the fun and the gang departed. Later that same day I faced a test of a much sterner nature.

The senior class had planned, and was in the process of producing, a public presentation of the dramatic version of *Gone With the Wind.* The proceeds would finance the class trip and each senior was expected to do his share in promoting the affair.

I had read the book during my pre-conversion days and found it fascinating. Now, my mind revolted at the thought of having anything to do with the project. Refusing to sell tickets to the event would make me very unpopular with the class. I climbed into the hayloft and wrestled with my God. Those sessions alone with the Lord confirmed my conviction that I must not accept tickets or attempt to sell them. The thought that other professing Christians in the class might join me, brought some comfort to my troubled mind.

During the activity period following the last class of the day, the senior president banged the gavel for attention.

"We have the tickets for the play," he announced. "I want each of you to take as many of the tickets as you think you can sell. I'll ask Joy and Ramona to start at opposite sides of the room and pass them out. Okay, girls."

Why do they always choose the prettiest, most popular girls for such tasks? Joy was pert, saucy, blonde and bubbly with friendliness. Ramona was dark, quiet, but beautiful. Joy started passing the tickets on my side of the room.

Hopefully, I watched as she approached Guy Lantz. He claimed to be a Christian and cheerfully served as class chaplain. He ought to reject the tickets. But, no! He asked for twenty! My heart sank to the bottom of my shoes.

Perhaps Don Jones . . . Don's father preached at the church where John, Nancy, and I had suffered much humiliation years before. Don belonged to that church; in fact, he made no secret of his activity as song leader and substitute teacher. But Don also accepted a sizeable lot of tickets.

"How many do you want, Kenneth?" Joy questioned with a beguiling smile.

"I'm sorry, Joy. I can't take any; I'm a Christian now." There, it was done. I had said it.

Angry color flooded Joy's face. "You stuffy old preacher!" she choked. "You'll spoil the fun for the rest of us." For ten seconds Joy stood immobile. Then her hand flashed in lightning swiftness. Its bite stung my cheek, but her words had cut deeper.

I cowered with embarrassment. The remainder of the seniors laughed in derision. When Joy saw that they were with her, she nonchalantly completed her assignment.

Very much discouraged, I trudged toward home. I desperately needed a place of solitude where I could talk in complete quiet with my God about the events of that day.

The bridge over Mill Creek offered such a place. The structure of the bridge was common in that area. The engineers utilized the abundant supply of stone to build the facility. It was high enough to sit under comfortably; at the same time its squatty nature and general position prevented anyone from seeing me from the road.

I laid my books under the floor boards on top of the rock foundation and sat down on the outcropping bridge abutment. My head sank between my knees as I gave way to dejection and self-pity.

Now discouragement is a sin and one of the Devil's prime tools, and self-pity God cannot tolerate in His children. He went to work to eradicate these from my thinking. He guided my attention back to His Word.

"Did you turn the other cheek?" He asked softly.

The other cheek? "Whosoever shall smite thee on thy right cheek, turn to him the other also." I'd forgotten! But the Lord wasn't through with me. He directed my mind to travel further. The same passage contained these words, "Blessed are ye, when men shall revile you, and persecute you, and shall say all manner of evil against you falsely, for my sake. Rejoice and be exceeding glad; for great is your reward in heaven."

With a much lighter step I left the solitude of the bridge. As I tramped over the frozen road and around the boulders, up and down the hills, my mind raced. I recalled that Peter and John rejoiced that they were counted worthy of suffering for Christ. That in turn reminded me that a slap in the face, some spiteful words, and derisive laughter, were minute in comparison to what Christ endured for me.

The truth struck like a ton of brick. All of these Christ had gone through before He died. But His suffering hadn't ended with a slap in the face, spiteful words, and laughter, as mine had; the *cross* followed. And here *I* was, moping . . .

I paused right in the middle of the road, confessing my guilt and seeking forgiveness for the sin of self-pity.

One of the best aids in combating discouragement is positive action. Before retiring to the attic with Vernon that evening, I reread Matthew 5. "Bless them that curse you and pray for those who despitefully use you and persecute you."

Joy, I concluded, had despitefully used me. The command jumped at me from the page of the Book. *Pray for Joy.* I did, that day, every day, many times each day as she entered my mind or as I passed her in the halls at school. And, Elijah's God is the same today and answers prayer in the same old way. I believed that then; I still do.

It is well, however, that I had no inkling of the method the Lord would employ in answering those petitions in Joy's behalf.

XI

REAPING

God's laws do not alter. He has said, "I am the Lord; I change not." It would be foolish to assume that we could spend years of our lives "sowing to the wind" without "reaping the whirlwind." Reap indeed we did.

That process touched us at a tender spot—the heart of our home—Mother.

I awoke groggily one blustery Friday night in late February, wondering what had roused me. I listened intently for a brief second. Dad's frantic voice brought me from my bed under the low eaves.

"Kenneth!" he called from the room below me. "Are you awake? Something is wrong with Mother!"

Hastily, for Dad's voice carried deep urgency, I grabbed a blanket from my bed and threw it around my shivering body. I climbed down the ladder into the girls' bedroom. Dad waited for me at the door into their room.

And indeed something was very much wrong. Mother slouched on the bed. Her vague, bewildered expression, coupled with the far away gleam in her eyes, denoted Mother's departure from reality. Her manner frightened me.

"What happened, Dad?" I asked.

He didn't have time to reply. Mother stood up tiredly. She walked barefoot toward the living room.

"Mother, where are you going?" Dad asked, taking her arm and bringing her carefully back to bed.

"Nancy! I must see about Nancy!" Mother sobbed. "She's hurt! Ralph, you don't want to leave her outside, do you?" Mother pleaded.

Dad turned hopelessly to me. I prayed earnestly for wisdom.

"Nancy is in her room asleep. She's all right, Mother. See?" I led her into the girls' room. With the resiliency of youth, they had slept through the entire episode.

"That isn't Nancy. That's Joyce. Nancy is outside hurt," Mother insisted, again heading for the door. "I must get to her and help her."

"Mother," I replied, catching her hand comfortingly, "Aunt Joyce, your sister, has been dead for years. Remember? She died with diptheria. This is Nancy."

"Oh," Mother replied carefully. Her mind seemed to be working more normally. "That is right. This must be Nancy."

Nancy's eyes flew open. "Well, of course I'm me!" she snapped irritably. "Who else would I be? Do you have to wake me in the middle of the night to tell me that?" She stared icily at the group surrounding the bed. Dark eerie shadows reflected against the walls and in the dark corners of the room from the candle Dad had lighted in the next room. Nancy glanced from Dad to me, to Mother. "What in the world is going on?"

I searched for words. Nancy wouldn't wait long for an explanation. Mother might be hurt deeply by her barbs, if I couldn't come up with a kind, sensitive reply. The Lord aided me. He placed the words in my mouth.

"Mother woke up confused, Nancy," I told her. "She thought you were out in the cold, hurt. She wanted to go out and help you. We had to show her that you were all right." With my eyes I beseeched Nancy to be kind, to be gentle, not to hurt Mother with her sharp tongue.

Surprisingly, Nancy placed a soft hand over Mother's rough calloused ones. "I'm fine, Mother. I'm right here. Go back to bed." She squeezed those worn hands lovingly and urged, "Go to bed and get your rest, Mother."

Obediently, Mother allowed Dad to steer her to their room. I waited until Dad extinguished the candle and the faint patch of light vanished. I wriggled my bulky frame through the attic opening and crept to bed.

"Oh, God! What has happened to Mother? Will she sleep now? How will she be in the morning? Can anything be done for her?" I prayed fervently as I mulled over the devastating scenes of the last hour. I faintly remembered a time in years past when Mother had experienced a similar breakdown. However, it had accompanied the death of an infant son. She had been so well in recent years, especially since she had come to know the Lord.

An event of the morning flashed into my thoughts.

"Kenneth," Mother had said immediately before breakfast, "I need an egg for lunches. Will you go to the chicken house and get one for me?"

"Sure, Mother, but it's early for the hens to be laying, and there weren't any last evening." I glanced out the kitchen window toward the pink-tinted sky, "It's hardly light yet," I said.

Mother smiled cheerfully, unruffled by my doubts. "You'll find some eggs, son. The Lord knows we need them, but Christ said ask, so I've asked. Now, run along quickly and bring them. Time is wasting."

Shaking my head in amazement, I had "run along quickly." Sure enough, I found two nice warm eggs in the nest. Mother took the eggs, added milk, flour, seasonings and made sandwiches for Nancy, Ellen, and me. Vernon was no longer in school.

And, now, this dear trusting Mother . . . Tears flooded my eyes as I talked to the Lord about her.

Saturday afternoon as Mother slept under the influence of a sedative, Dr. Todd spoke to Dad and Brother Lightfoot, who had joined us following a desperate message through Dad's employer, and my Aunt Mabel, Dad's sister.

"There is nothing we can do," Dr. Todd informed Dad. "Too much stress at some point in her life . . . or nervous tension and frustration . . . Her constitution and mental makeup weren't strong enough to stand the strain." His words shocked us into silence. We couldn't say a word. I scrutinized my shoes while guilty memories scrambled through my mind. Although I dared not look at Dad, I knew certainly that his conscience pricked just as sharply as mine. Dr. Todd misunderstood our silence. He studied us sympathetically. "She has lived in great stress, has she not?" he prodded.

Dad nodded brokenly. "Is there . . ." he stammered, and tried again. "I've known folks who . . . who . . . . Will she, maybe, try to, to . . ."

"Take her own life?" the doctor kindly supplied.

Dad nodded his head. The thought hadn't occurred to me. Mentally, I jumped to attention.

"No, not with this type of mental disturbance," the doctor comforted. "You'll find her either distressed or disoriented. Sometimes she may be almost normal for a time. Just treat her with love and understanding."

"We'll be praying," Brother Albert promised, gripping our hands with deep sympathy, "Have faith in God, friends."

Aunt Mabel sniffed disdainfully as Brother Lightfoot departed; her words haunted me for years, "Just wait, you'll all end up in the crazy house. Just wait and see."

True to the doctor's prediction, Mother's condition varied widely. I sorely missed her gentle smile on those evenings when all too frequently I arrived home to find her in tears. Even more distressing than this was Mother's inability to think and to pray with us, and to offer us wise counsel for those ever-present problems. She no longer sang softly as she tidied up the house after we were in bed. This silence depressed me strangely. Yes, I had Dad, and I thanked the Lord for him. But even the most considerate Christian father cannot fill a Mother's place in the home.

With Mother's illness much of the responsibility shifted into the hands of the men. Nancy should have accepted the role of housekeeper, but any attempt to persuade her of this produced such violent scenes that we gave it up. She did, grudgingly, give Ellen some matronly attention. Vernon, in his simple way, still seemed to feel responsible for Ellen. He helped her with her reading. He also acted as her playmate. They found romping outdoors with our collie great fun. Vernon had also learned to split wood; he loved the chore. Ellen sat on a stump, watching the chips fly, until Vernon stopped. Together they filled the woodbox. They soon forgot that life in our home, and Mother, had been different.

Nancy's rebellion grew. In her better moments Mother worried about Nancy. Dad and I comforted Mother by assuring her that God would hear and answer our prayers for Nancy.

Meanwhile, in spite of heartbreak and sorrow, life must go on. Almost four months remained in the school year. When the day ended, my mind returned to Mother. How would she be? Depressed? Confused? Living in the past, in those days before trouble and sorrow weighted her so heavily?

The whole family prayed for Mother's recovery. My altar under the bridge saw much service in those days as I prayed desperately, "Dear God, must it be this way? Must it always be this way? How will Mother be this evening? Will she be well enough to read the Bible for us once again, will she . . . ? But already, other concerns entered my mind. I thought of the future, "And, oh dear Lord, isn't there someone, somewhere, to fill this awful, empty gap in my life?"

During February, snow blusters frequently in those Pennsylvania hills. I knelt by my bed as the snow whistled under the eaves. "Lord, isn't there someone, somewhere in this world for me?"

XII

OLD SCAR HEALED

Mother's illness did not erase my concern for Joy. I continued to pray for her, often pausing under the bridge in the evening to speak with my God about her soul. Nevertheless, I'm sure that if I had known how God would answer my prayers for Joy, I would not have prayed so fervently in her behalf.

It happened this way. Joel Adams, who was Joy's steady at the time, came to me May 15 and said, "Kenneth, Joy is in the hospital at Lucas. She's very ill; the doctors aren't expecting her to live. She keeps calling for you. I know how you must feel," he shuffled uncomfortably—"but will you go to see her?" The warning bell jangled for class.

"Of course I will," I replied. "What seems to be her trouble?"

Joel glanced down the long hall; a few stragglers dribbled into room 20, the scene of his class. "I don't have time to explain now," Joel replied, dashing down the corridor. I raced to American History, praying earnestly for Joy's life as I ran.

Rather reluctantly, I walked the extra three miles to Lucas. This meant a six-mile walk to return to the school. That, added to the first three, made a nine-mile trek home. But, for the sake of a soul . . .

I wasn't the only visitor to the Lucas hospital that evening. As I set foot on the porch of the building, a "Leaping Lena" tin Lizzie, or Model A Ford, full of hilarious young people also arrived. The vehicle carried such colorful slogans as "Give 'em the axe" and "Let 'em have it." (Today's version would be, "Sock it to 'em.") Even Joel who drove the car, seemed to be having a high time.

I entered the building and located Joy's room. As I approached the door, a lady came out. She identified herself as Mrs. Jones, Joy's mother.

"Come in. My daughter keeps calling for you," she invited.

Laughter drifted to us from the upper end of the hall. Mrs. Jones paused with her hand on the door. A frown passed briefly over her face as she recognized Joel and Joy's friends.

"Shall we go in?" she asked.

"Yes," I responded.

Joy lay in the white hospital bed, very pallid, almost the

picture of death itself. She stirred at our entrance and new life glimmered in her suffering, frightened eyes.

"Oh, you've come at last!" she cried feebly.

"It's all right; don't try to talk," I began, but to Joy my visit meant life or death, and she wasn't interested in dying. She wouldn't be discouraged from talking until she had said what she wanted to say. Frankly, her request wasn't quite what I had expected to hear.

Joy extended a limp hand. I clasped it gently. At that moment Joel and his friends halted in the corridor outside the open door.

"Well," I heard Joel whisper loudly to the other youth, "I see the preacher kept his promise. He's here." The young man and his lady friend giggled noisily.

"I thought preachers always kept their promises—to avoid the 'hot house,' you know," the second youth wisecracked.

Disgusted with their lack of fear and reverence for the things of God, I closed my ears as best I could. Joy was speaking again. I stooped to catch her words.

"I knew you'd come," she said. "They don't expect me to live. Will you pray for me? When you talk to God, he hears." She paused to gather strength. "Will you please put your hands upon my head and pray for me?"

"Of course I will, Joy," I replied while tears threatened my own composure.

Reverent quietness reigned in the hall when I placed my work-roughened hands on Joy's white forehead. I beseeched the Lord for her physical health, but also, for her spiritual well-being. I prayed for her mother and her friends beyond the open door. As I prayed, I sensed my Lord's nearness; I knew that He would heal Joy's body, and that she, too, would acknowledge Him as Lord and Saviour.

When I removed my hands, it seemed to those observing that already God was at work. And why should it not be so? He has promised, "Before they call, I will answer and while they are yet speaking, I will hear."

I wanted to speak to Joy about her need to accept Christ, but common sense warned that now wasn't the time. The Father had spared her life. Either I, or some other child of His would be given that opportunity when she was physically stronger. Joy did accept Christ sometime later. She and her husband (not Joel) became dear friends of our family.

I prepared to leave, promising Joy to visit her again, if possible. "Even if I can't come back, I'll pray for you," I assured her. The young people in the hall slipped into the room as Mrs. Jones accompanied me to the door.

"What is wrong with Joy?" I asked Mrs. Jones, as we stood outside the door.

"I'm not sure if I can explain," Mrs. Jones answered. "The doctors say it's an infection from old scar tissue. She had an accident several years ago, the wounds of which healed very slowly. It may stem from that." Tears flooded her eyes. "You will come back?"

"I'll try to."

"And you will keep praying for her?"

"Yes."

Hurrying, I retraced my steps to Milltown, and thence homeward. How I longed to stop under the bridge for a heart to heart talk with my Lord. But, glancing at the sun sinking ever lower in the sky, I knew I couldn't spare the time. With Dad working on a farm, our chores fell on my shoulders. And Nancy—even with Mother's illness—Nancy refused to perform cheerfully any home responsibility. So, to maintain peace for Mother's well-being, Dad and I often stepped in and did the odd jobs that needed to be done.

"Don't you think it's time you opened your heart to Christ, Nancy?" I asked late that evening. Dad, Mother, and the younger ones had retired. I tried to study, but Joy's white features and Nancy's sullen expression as she hunched over her books prevented it.

"Why should I? What has religion done for Mother?" she snapped, slamming her history book shut.

"Oh, Nancy!" I said sorrowfully. "Don't you remember what home was like before Christ came into our lives? The drinking, the anger, the swearing, the damning, and all that? Don't you remember?"

"Yes. But look at Mother now! I don't want anything to do with a God who'll do to Mother what her God has done to her. Forget it!"

"Oh, but you're wrong, Nancy! God didn't do it. We did."

"We did!" Nancy's eyes popped. "What in the world do you mean by that?"

"Those years," I tried to explain, "of bootlegging, drinking, and carousing were too much for Mother. Her health gave way because of the strain. We were responsible for it, because Mother wanted nothing to do with home brew. She begged us not to go into the business, and not to drink the stuff. In spite of everything she said, we went ahead. Now we're reaping."

"Reaping?" Nancy asked timidly.

"Be not deceived, God is not mocked. For whatsoever a man soweth, that shall he also reap," I quoted. "It's true, Nancy. I visited a girl in the hospital this evening who is reap . . ."

"Forget it," Nancy interrupted. "I don't want to hear about it." She snarled savagely, "I plan to have a good time with my life. If there is a God, I'll think about Him later—after I've had my fun."

Nancy pushed aside her books and went to bed. Preoccupied, I idly flipped the pages of the large green book. Startled, the problems of the present faded as I studied the maps spread over those pages.

A scene from the past replaced my concerns of the present. "What are those squiggly blue lines?" Nancy had asked.

"Lakes," I had replied.

And now, as then, a strange power seemed to draw me to that land of lakes and muskeg.

XIII

LORETTA? SUSIE?

As I trudged home from school that evening in early June, my mind was occupied with tomorrow's examinations, graduation, my impending job on Mr. Cook's farm, and a multitude of other things. For once, no thoughts of home and its frustrating problems troubled me.

When I stepped up on the porch, the aroma of baking bread wafted to my nostrils. "Oh, has Nancy decided to bake, once?" I wondered to myself. Then I heard someone singing. That definitely was *not* Nancy's voice singing praises to God. Unbelievingly, I paused to listen, to be sure. Yes, unlikely as it seemed Mother had recovered her mental balance. She had set the house in order, baked, and began preparations for supper. How we praised the Lord!

All of us except Nancy, that is. She found no reason to praise Him. To her, Mother's recovery was just a happy coincidence.

Following graduation, I moved to Lucas where I assisted Brother Cook on his dairy farm. Nancy, who had ideas and plans of her own, left the responsibility for the house largely to Mother. Although mentally stable, Mother lacked the physical strength necessary for heavy household chores. I walked home each weekend and helped her clean and do the laundry.

While at home, I always joined Mother and Dad on Sunday at Oberlin Mission. This Sunday, Allen Martz announced that he would soon be leaving the mission. I found the news devastating.

"But, Kenneth," he reasoned, "there are plenty of people here in the east to bring the gospel to needy persons. Out in Minnesota the Indians have no one to tell them of Christ. The Lord has called; I must go."

I remembered the wordless call I had experienced. I knew whereof he spoke. "Of course you must," I agreed. "The Lord be with you and Sister Betsy. We'll miss you here, though."

"I'm sure you will," Brother Allen nodded. It was a simple acknowledgement of fact. "Jonas Miller is an excellent teacher, a man of the Word. He'll soon more than fill my shoes," Brother Allen added.

Brother Jonas proved to be a very capable teacher, truly a man of God. He was single, and not too many years older than I.

One Sunday we arrived at the mission to find a slender black-haired girl standing beside Brother Jonas on the porch. He introduced her to us as "Loretta Martin, my fiancee."

Something about Sister Loretta impressed me deeply. Perhaps it was the depth of her spiritual understanding which became evident during our class discussion. Or it may have been her very real love for the neglected waifs of the hills.

But, while these virtues struck me, as I think back to those days, the thing that impressed me most was the love and understanding shared by Jonas and Loretta. Often this understanding expressed itself in a gentle smile that flashed between them. I had never seen anything like it before. I longed for someone who would share my joys as Loretta did with Jonas. She seemed to sense his moods, even to anticipate his reaction to varying circumstances.

Well, whatever that elusive quality may have been, I heard myself pleading as I walked back to the Cook farm that evening, "Dear God, isn't there someone in the world like Sister Loretta for me? Someone like Sister Loretta to share the joys and sorrows of life with me? Isn't there, dear Lord?"

Let me emphasize: I hadn't fallen in love with Loretta Martin. My feeling for her was limited to deep respect. She belonged to Jonas Miller and I had no desire to change that. I knew the Lord was able to provide a wife for me who possessed those inner qualities evident in Loretta. That was all I asked of my Lord—a girl like Sister Loretta. Jonas and Loretta married that same summer.

God does take us literally!

Two years and many pleas later, I attended a youth meeting in the home of Brother Albert Lightfoot. As I entered the living room the presence of a young woman startled me. Sister Loretta! But where was Jonas? I searched the room visually but couldn't see him anywhere.

"Kenneth, I want you to meet our visitor," Brother Albert said, steering me toward the young woman. "The rest of the group have met her."

"Susie, this is Kenneth Eagle from the Oberlin Mission," Albert said amiably. "Kenneth, meet Susie Lantz, from the Townsend church."

I can't describe how I felt. Here was a young woman almost the exact copy of Sister Loretta! After an awkward silence, I found my tongue.

"You look so very much like a young woman in our congregation," I informed her.

"Oh? Who is she?" Susie asked with live curiosity.

"Loretta Martin Miller, wife of Jonas Miller. Do you know her?"

"No. Isn't it strange? I've never heard of her," Susie replied. "We must not know the same people."

That evening we discussed II Timothy and during the lesson the subject of persecution came forward. The conversation turned to the reformation period, and the many martyrs of that era. This interested me immensely because it was fresh and new. I hadn't heard the stories of Martin Luther and Menno Simons over and over as many of our young people have.

"Susie," Brother Albert encouraged, "tell us about your grandfather—how many greats is it?"

Susie chuckled quietly. "I'm not certain, Brother Lightfoot. But I'll gladly tell the story, if you think it won't bore the group. Some of them have heard it before, I'm sure."

"I haven't," I said impulsively. "Please tell us." Susie's eyes roved questioningly around the table. The remainder of the gathering nodded agreement.

"Well, his name was Hans Landes and he was the last of the martyrs in Switzerland. For his refusal to recant his stand on believers' baptism, he was placed on a galley ship and chained to an oar. Somehow he escaped. When the authorities caught him again, they decided to take no chances. With a rope around his neck he was led to the chopping block."

Susie paused. Quietness that could be felt surrounded us. She picked up the narrative, "With his last breath before the executioner severed his head from his body, he admonished his family to be faithful."

Someone like Sister Loretta! Elation filled me as I trudged in our lane that moonlit night. I knew beyond a doubt that God had answered my prayers. But, could Susie accept the attentions of an uncultured backward young man from the hills? She had grown up on a neat well-kept farm among gentle, educated, and well-mannered people. Would the cultural gap between us be too great? Her ancestors for many generations were Christians. Mine? I shuddered as I recalled our all too recent past. Doubts flooded my mind.

I sought my old refuge, the Thousand Acre Woodland. There, on my knees, my Lord brought reassurance. "You asked; I answered!" He seemed to say. "Now, just follow as I lead."

Later, Susie told me of an experience she had the next day. "I was in Philadelphia shopping," she said, "when an elderly lady greeted me. 'Hello, Loretta!' she said. 'Oh, I'm not Loretta

was my wife's neat, orderly appearance—but he finally said, "Well, I wouldn't rent to just any young couple, but I will to you." We were jubilant.

We had little furniture, but we really didn't need much. The grounds surrounding our "home" had been stomped and trampled by many feet and any existing vegetation had perished long ago. Friends offered us roots, and sprouts of their prized perennials, and seeds. Our yard soon blossomed with beauty and our home became our pride and joy. Sometimes, in our preoccupation with making that house a home, we almost forgot our fear of being separated.

We weren't allowed to forget the war very long at any time, though. The railroad traversed the valley below our house. From our kitchen window Susie watched as it transported long car loads of army equipment—tanks, artillery, or machine guns. Sometimes, instead of equipment, the engines pulled coach cars carrying personnel. Either served as a grim reminder of a nation at war.

I didn't need to see the trains to be reminded. The progress of the conflict seemed to be the chief topic of conversation among the customers entering the store. My own prospects for the future weighed heavily on my mind. If I trudged home along the railroad tracks—depressed—Susie knew without asking what bothered me.

One day in August a letter arrived from Uncle Sam containing a questionnaire. I filled in the form and returned it.

Again uncertainty hounded us. Should we give up our home? Would it be wise for Susie to seek a job? Ought she return to her father's home, or try to keep our little nest? Before we had reached a decision, a new complication developed. We discovered that we were expectant parents.

Our uncertainties were still unresolved when I received another letter instructing me to appear for my physical examination.

Susie and I had received no direct leading from the Lord in solving our problems. We could only wait, believing that He held the solution and would reveal it in His time.

Never did we suspect the area wherein our Father's solution lay. The examining doctor listened to my heart and checked my blood pressure. He shook his head, puzzled.

"Sit down here for awhile, young man," he told me. "I want to check you further a little later."

Unconcerned, I did as the doctor said. Again, the physician adjusted the arm band, squeezed the bulb, and listened to the stethoscope. Again he shook his head in bewilderment. He marked my form 4F—or physically unfit—and turned me loose.

Being classified "unfit" almost jolted my wife and me. I had always considered myself extremely healthy; I was never ill, and took a hard day's work in stride. It was somewhat discomfiting to realize that I might not be as well as I had always supposed myself to be. Susie was a little concerned, but if this was the price we needed to pay to avoid an unknown period of separation, we accepted it willingly, and praised the Lord for it. We committed my health to the Lord.

My brother, John, encouraged by my good "fortune," now married his sweetheart, Joan, and moved back to Philadelphia where he had a good job.

We were happy in our little home. Although we were spared from separation, our home soon no longer belonged exclusively to us. Father asked us to share it with Vernon, who had become too much of a burden for Mother, who was suffering with asthma and a heart condition.

It was well that we could not see further into the future.

XV

OLD ROB

A magnificent surprise awaited us at Oberlin Mission that first Sunday in May. We arrived early. When Susie and I walked in together, a head of familiar red hair startled us. Moreover, a neat white prayer veiling covered that tidily combed hair. The owner of that fiery head could be only one individual.

"Cousin Cass!" I exclaimed joyfully.

And indeed, Cousin Cass had found the Lord. How we praised Him! She looked so sweet, almost like an angel. Many of the hard lines had vanished from her face as the joy of the Lord filled her heart. In the service, her voice rang above those around her; she had been redeemed from so much.

"Where are you living, Kenneth?" Cousin Cass asked, as we chatted after the service.

"In the old Stoneburg schoolhouse," I replied. "I've worked in a grocery store in Stoneburg for several years."

Brother Albert shook hands with us at the door and issued an invitation. "I'm going into the hills to visit Old Rob today. Will you all go along?" He added, "Bring Vernon with you. We'll have room for him."

Susie looked at me, indicating the decision should be mine. We had nothing planned for the afternoon to prevent us from joining Albert and Sally.

"We'll be glad to go, Brother Albert," I responded. "Shall we meet you here?"

"Yes. At about 1:30?"

"Fine!"

Dad cornered us as my wife and I started toward our car. "I want to talk to you, Kenneth," he said soberly.

We stopped and waited. "Sure, Dad. Is something wrong?"

"W-e-l-l, in a way, yes," Dad faltered. "Mother's asthma and heart are so bad, she can hardly look after herself, much less Ellen. Could you and Susie keep Ellen until Mother's health improves?" He hated to ask—I could see that—but knowing Mother's frail condition, I realized he had no choice. Susie listened sympathetically.

I glanced at my wife questioningly. "Of course we'll take her, Father Eagle," Susie replied. "How will we arrange to pick her up, Kenneth?"

"We'll drop by for her after visiting Old Rob, Dad," I replied. "Probably about 4:30."

"Old Rob, huh?" Dad grunted. He scratched his head doubtfully. "Well, the Lord saved me," he declared after a moment's meditation, "I guess He can Rob, too."

My thoughts reverted to Old Rob as we drove out of the hills into Stoneburg for lunch. "I've known him for years," I remarked to my wife. "He chews tobacco like a hog." Incidentally—that is the only way people do chew it! "When we were children, he spit the juice on our bare toes. We hated the old man." I could still see in my mind's eye the tobacco juice dribbling down his stubbly beard and sniff the ever present odor of corn whiskey. He brewed his own and drank a quart of the stuff a day. His language, for filth and foulness, could scarcely be equaled. At first, he had been rather rude to Albert, but this attitude had changed.

"How does he make a living?" Susie wondered.

"He's a woodcutter—the best in the hills," I replied, recalling Rob's ability to swing a double-bitted axe. "I guess he must be as good as Abe Lincoln."

"I'm anxious to meet him," Susie said eagerly.

"His home won't be like the homes you've seen in the hills," I warned.

"I'm sure of that," Susie acknowledged. "Don't worry, Kenneth. The Lord will take care of everything. Just trust Him. Okay?"

Susie had visited my home frequently during our courtship. Although still very poor by city standards, it exceeded the quality of many hill homes. Nancy, compelled by my absence, accepted responsibility with Mother for its cleanliness.

We met Brother Albert and Sally Lightfoot at the mission. Albert's car, the same blue Plymouth sedan which he had driven down our boulder-strewn lane some years before, now wound up a narrow rocky road, carrying the message of God's love to another neglected soul.

"People—even some of our own church folks—tell me to forget Rob," Albert sorrowfully informed me. He, Vernon an ' I occupied the front seat; conversation was simpler for all of us that way. "You know, Kenneth, he has come forward at our last two series of meetings, but each time his bottle won the victory and he slipped back. I'm convinced," Albert emphasized his statement, "that our God is able and will bring Rob to true repentance."

Chuckling, Albert turned to face my wife. "Susie, you'll have to ask Sally about the day we invited Rob to our house for supper."

"Oh?" Susie inquired. "How about it, Sally?"

Albert's mischievous chuckle pricked our curiosity. As I turned to face Sally to better catch her story, the many delicate tulip poplar blossoms caught my attention. The woods gleamed with color.

"Well," Sally began, "we brought Rob to our home for supper one evening last fall and took him to revivals afterward. I had made a dish of orange pudding . . ."

"It's an old family recipe—handed down for generations," Albert interrupted.

"I make it for special occasions," Sally added, continuing her recital, "such as Christmas or birthdays. I also fixed several other special dishes, such as roast beef and gravy, mashed potatoes, cole slaw—you know—Susie—the usual company meal."

Susie nodded her understanding. I knew she was picturing her aunt's table, complete with all the "company" fixings.

"What did Rob do," Sally continued, "but take a dip of each dish—gravy, meat, pudding and all—mix them all together on his plate, and eat them with one big swish!" We gasped with wonder.

Sally laughed. "At the time," she grinned, "it was rather deflating to my ego! I always considered myself a good cook!"

". . . and you are!" Susie comforted.

Albert took up the recital of that memorable day. "You were at revivals that evening, weren't you, Kenneth?"

"Yes," I replied. "Quite a few eyebrows lifted askance when you brought him in. I heard one person behind me whisper, 'Why does he bother with that filthy bum? He can't do without his bottle . . .'"

"And one man moved to another bench upon some pretense, because he was afraid of bedbugs," Sally added.

"Bedbugs!" Susie ejaculated, lifting an eyebrow of her own. She thought we were joking.

"Really!" Sally protested. "We've seen them crawling on his clothing."

"Well!" my wife sputtered. "If God could protect Daniel from the lions, He surely can protect us from a little old bed bug, can't He?"

"I guess the brother didn't think that far, Susie," Brother Albert replied, smiling broadly. He negotiated a sharp, rock-bound curve, and the vehicle emerged into an open, weed-cluttered clearing. Tall thistles sporting beautiful purple flowers edged the grassy lane.

We soon tested Susie's theory—or rather—her faith. Albert parked the sedan beside an old, abandoned hen coop. Even before we left the car, the overpowering stench of the place almost nauseated us. I almost felt like throwing up, which would have been most embarrassing!

Inside the coop we found Rob, living among the hen house furnishings: nests—replete with china nest eggs; water fountains; feeders, and other poultry equipment. The ladies took the only "chairs" (two empty wooden crates) while Albert and I sat with Rob on the bed, being keenly aware of the possibility of "varmints" as we did so! Before we left that day, Rob had made a new commitment to Christ. He handed his liquor bottle and remaining supply of that product to Albert.

"Get rid of it! I never want to smell the stuff again," he said. "I've got something better now. And the 'baccur.'" He dug a grimy pouch from his hip pocket and gave it to our friend. "I won't need this, either." We were delighted with the assignment of disposing of both products.

As I watched Brother Albert tuck the bottle and pouch into a paper bag, my mind reverted to this babe in Christ and the help he would need to grow spiritually. "Can you read, Brother Rob?" I asked, remembering the New Testament in my pocket.

"No," he said sorrowfully. "I was too busy helpin' Pa bootleg to go to school much. I niver larned to read."

"You read a chapter for us before we go, Kenneth," Brother Albert suggested.

I prayed for guidance. I knew that Susie was also praying. I chose to read Colossians 3, explaining the sense of the passage as I read, and aided by Albert's comments.

"You all be sure to come back," our host urged, as we departed.

"I'll come by for you Sunday morning," Brother Lightfoot promised. "Don't forget to talk to the Lord every day, Rob," he called as he backed the sedan around. Our host smiled and waved happily.

"I believe he'll make it this time," my friend rejoiced. "It's the first time he has voluntarily given up his bottle and tobacco. He'll need lots of nurture, though."

"Why don't we drop by one evening this week?" I asked.

"Fine!" Albert agreed. "I was going to ask if you could."

We halted at a spot where the absence of boulders permitted us to leave the roadway, and parked the vehicle. With prayerful gratitude, not only for Rob's deliverance from alcohol but also for my own, I up-ended the bottle and allowed the sparkling amber fluid to drain to the ground. The contents of the tobacco pouch Brother Albert tossed to the mercy of the four winds; a westerly breeze scattered the dark fragments thither and yon.

Truly, as our joy overflowed, there must also have been great rejoicing among the angels in Heaven.

Susie and I stopped at my old home place for Ellen and her personal belongings before returning to our schoolhouse home.

"Where's Nancy, Dad?" I inquired, failing to see my sixteen-year-old sister anywhere.

"Out somewhere with Joe Jones," Dad replied heavily. He sighed, "I'm afraid that lad is no good; he will bring her nothing but trouble, but she won't listen to any one." I nodded soberly. I knew just what Dad was talking about.

My heart ached for Mother. Dad took care of her the best he could, but she needed expert care and balanced meals which Dad was not qualified to provide. But what could we do? Already, our small house overflowed with residents!

XVI

BACK INTO THE HILLS

Brother Albert and I visited Rob on Tuesday evening. To our amazement, he quoted almost verbatim Colossians 3, which I had read for him on our previous visit. He held another surprise for us. He insisted upon learning to read, so he could peruse the Word of God for himself.

Albert and I stared doubtfully at each other. Rob was nearly eighty years of age, and his eyesight poor.

"Very well," Albert promised, when it appeared the aged man would not be deterred. "We'll try, Rob. My children have some first grade primers. That's where we'll need to start."

"Good, good!" Brother Rob replied, almost clapping his hands with joy. The seed we had sown was bringing forth fruit. As usually happens, the regeneration of the inner man resulted as well in the cleansing of his physical surroundings. Rob had attempted to remove the filth from his hovel; nevertheless, the stench remained. We appreciated his effort. (We later saw this same principle demonstrated over and over again among the Indians in the Northland.)

A few days later, Sally Lightfoot called Susie while I was at work. "Albert is ill. He promised to visit Luke and Lilly Lucifer over beyond Milltown. Could you and Kenneth go for us?"

"I'm almost sure we can, but I'll have to check with Kenneth," my wife answered. "I'll call you back, Sally."

Of course we accepted the pinch-hitting assignment. The long summer evening lingered as our 1932 Chevrolet bounced through the trees and over the narrow rock-cluttered roads. Lengthening shadows mottled the forest as the sun crept toward the western horizon. My heart ached to be back among these hills of home.

We located the Lucifer residence. It perched atop a steep hill, back away from the road. Several neglected chicken houses stood at the edge of the clearing. Two others sat in a depression below the asbestos-shingled barn. A small garden plot studded with last years' dead sweet-corn stalks, and overgrown with weeds, lay between those chicken coops and the Lucifer lane.

We enjoyed our chat with Luke and Lilly. I read the Word for them and led in prayer. I remarked, as we prepared to leave,

"You must have good soil here, judging by the height of the corn in your last year's garden."

"Yes," Luke agreed, "but I can't manage the place anymore. A young person can make a good living on a place like this. We have thought of moving out."

The drive home reminded me of the night of my conversion. The full moon gleamed overhead; fluffy white clouds floated lazily in a deep purple sky. Susie shared my wonder and delight in the beauty of the night.

At home again, my wife said, "I like those hills; they're really beautiful."

"Yes," I agreed, my heart beating frantically. "Sometimes I wish we could live there." Often I had felt the Lord calling me back to those hills, but had never mentioned it to Susie.

"Oh, I'm so glad!" Susie rejoiced. "I've been waiting to hear you say that. I wish we could go tomorrow!"

Together we told the Lord about it. If He wanted us in the hills, He would provide the place, and the means of making a living. We had no doubt but that this was God's will. The question was, "When, and where?"

Yet, that query had already been answered! The solution dawned suddenly as we discussed the matter at the supper table the next evening.

"The Lucifer place, Kenneth! They were thinking of leaving. Remember?" Susie asked excitedly.

I dropped my fork. "Of course! That must be why the Lord took us up there," I marvelled. Impulsively, I suggested, "Let's drive out there."

"Now?" Susie asked.

"Of course!"

"We'll do the dishes first," my practical Susie insisted. She washed, Ellen wiped, and soon we were on the way.

The Lord reaffirmed our faith as we turned into the Lucifer property. A large "For Sale" sign kindled our spirits to the bursting point. This was it! How we praised the Lord for His infallible leading.

Well, soon we found ourselves and our impromptu family living on the fourteen-acre Lucifer farm, purchased with a loan from the bank in the form of a mortgage on the property.

Since we now lived much nearer to Brother Rob than Albert Lightfoot did, I became his tutor in his reading instruction. What pleasure to hear again, "See Jane run. See Dick run. Funny, funny Dick. Funny, funny Jane."

We progressed to "The ball is red," and "See the blue car. See the blue car run." Although Rob worked valiantly, he never accomplished much with reading. Nevertheless, his ability to retain what he had heard thrilled us. We read numerous precious Bible selections for him and shared rich and rewarding hours around the Word of God. John 14 became his favorite choice.

Prostate gland trouble forced Rob to abandon his hen coop for hospital residence. He never fully recovered from surgery. Because he had no physical relatives to claim his body, it was taken 150 miles away to a place where it would be used in medical research. Some of the brethren didn't object.

"He had no family and what is learned will benefit society as a whole," they argued. "Besides, what can we do about it?"

Brother Albert didn't agree with the decision. "No," he declared, "we are his family in the Lord. You wouldn't want this to be done to one of your brothers, would you? He is our brother. We must bring him back for burial."

So, one windy, stormy night when the rain poured down in torrents, our dear brother Albert went after the body of Brother Rob. He drove that same old blue sedan with the black fenders in which he had come seeking us, and brought back the body of our brother.

The memorial service at Oberlin Mission spoke so deeply of love and concern. Albert Lightfoot was "just" a layman, but, if it hadn't been for Albert, would our departed friend have become our brother? And even of more concern to Susie and me. What would have become of the Eagle family? Where would they be now, had it not been for Albert Lightfoot?

As Rob's body descended into the earth, I breathed an urgent prayer. "Lord, give me the tender compassion of Brother Albert."

The Lord began immediately to teach His pupil that lesson. Nancy, only sixteen years of age, eloped with Joe Jones. Dad found he could no longer care for Mother, who was bedfast, so we moved her into our home where Susie nursed her.

Mother enjoyed our hill home. "Oh, how beautiful!" she would exclaim as she lay propped up in bed near a window. "It reminds me of my girlhood home."

One evening when Mother felt unusually ill, and thinking that perhaps she might not live through the night, she called Susie and me to her bedside. She asked us to kneel beside the bed. Placing a hand on each of our heads, she said, "I don't have any money to leave you, but I can leave you the blessing of the Lord."

Mother prayed, asking the Lord's blessing, guidance and

direction for each of us and for our children. In the years since, that prayer has become very precious to me. I recall vividly an experience in Northern Minnesota when I had no money . . . but that is another part of the story.

However, Mother's health improved and she returned home. But then another crisis developed. John received his induction notice.

"This is the last time I'll see you, John," Mother said tearfully as he bid her good-bye. That parting brought sorrow because John had never accepted Christ as his Saviour.

John laughed at Mother's premonition, but it proved correct. Dad found Mother dead on the floor when he came into the house one morning several weeks later. John arrived home from Fort Eustis, Virginia, for his first furlough at noon of the same day to find Mother gone. It shook him profoundly.

Baby Michael entered our home soon after Mother's death. Shortly after this momentous event, John departed for overseas duty and Joan spent much of her time with us. She truly shared life with him across the miles during those long months.

Our family had grown by leaps and bounds. Within two years of our marriage our household consisted of six people—Susie and myself, Ellen, Vernon, Baby Michael, and Joan.

Vernon's presence in our home now brought unexpected rewards. His strong body proved a great asset in caring for our eight hundred Rhode Island Red laying hens. We carried all the water from the well, and this was quite a chore.

He also relieved us of the tiresome chore of lawn mowing. Something about that noisy contrivance fascinated him. He thoroughly enjoyed operating it, although it had to be pushed by hand. He also wielded a hoe in our garden crops, such as sweet corn and potatoes, which we marketed in Oberlin, Milltown, and Stoneburg. We also produced apples and berry crops, such as raspberries for market, but Vernon's disability prohibited him from doing much to help along this line.

It was a good life. As Luke Lucifer had said, "A young man can make a living on this place." We weren't getting rich, but our physical needs were being met. Perhaps we were in danger of becoming lazy and complacent. Whatever the reason, the Lord proceeded to deal with us in some of the most unexpected ways.

I had never shared with Susie my deep sense of call from the Lord. He set about changing this. One lovely summer morning my wife and I labored together picking the sweet, juicy raspberries in our patch on the Lucifer place. Susie had begun at the north end of the first row, while I started picking at the south end of the same row. The Lord spoke to me as the berries plunked into my bucket.

"Tell Susie that I'm calling you to the ministry," the Lord prodded. I hedged, "You haven't actually called me to the ministry, Lord, have you?" That still small voice repeated, "Tell your wife I'm calling you into my work, into the ministry."

I debated the issue as Susie and I approached each other from opposite sides of the raspberry patch. Knowing that joy and victory in Christian living hinge solely on obedience, I decided to take the plunge.

A strange but wonderful thing happened! As I opened my mouth to speak, Susie also opened hers. The same words issued from both our lips. They were, "Did you ever feel that the Lord was calling you to His work?"

While the Lord had been speaking to me, He had also been talking to Susie. I reluctantly told her of that wordless call I had experienced years before as a youth on the old home place. Even now, although I knew beyond a doubt that the Lord had His finger on us for a special purpose, I wasn't quite convinced my calling would be to the ministry.

Praise the Lord! He is patient with His faltering children. I think my disquieting experience with neighbor Jacob must have been another step in our "education." Whatever you prefer to call it, it caught me entirely off balance, unprepared.

XVII

"SPEAK TO JACOB"

Soon after our move to the hills, we encountered our neighbors, Jacob, Violet, and Jimmie Petit. They lived within shouting distance below us, under the hill. Our fourteen acres bordered their wooded lot on three sides. A short path connected the two houses.

My first meeting with Jacob occurred following our second trip off the hill to church. As we returned home, Jacob abandoned his car, parking it along the road below their house. He staggered toward the gate, reeling and swaying precariously. I drove slowly, watching to be sure that he reached the house without falling. He did.

The following Monday I found myself in need of a putty knife to fix some windows in the hen coops. I trudged down to Jacob's, on the chance he might own such a tool.

"Hello," I greeted Jacob, who peered uncertainly at me from under the hood of his car. "I'm Kenneth Eagle, your neighbor on the hill."

Without replying, Jacob continued to tighten spark plugs. I tried again. "Are you having car trouble, Mr. Petit?"

"No. Jake will do," the young man replied curtly.

I ignored his rudeness. "Can I help you with anything, Jacob? Could I assist you in getting your car out on the road?" It remained where he had left it on Sunday. However, I had been too preoccupied at that time with our neighbor's condition to notice that the vehicle was in the ditch.

Jacob turned to ponder the location of his car. "You can try," he grunted, eyeing my height and hefty build. He slammed the hood unceremoniously, turned the wheels to the proper position, and both of us pushed. With much effort, we succeeded in dislodging the car from the mud.

"Now," Jacob said, when that was done and the Ford had been parked at the front gate, "what do you want from me? It must be something."

Taken by surprise, I'm afraid my mouth dropped open. I stammered, "I-I- I merely wondered if you have a putty knife I could borrow for an hour or so."

"I'm afraid I don't," he replied, and stalked into the yard and up the steps to the house.

Susie fared better with Violet, Jacob's wife, and little Jimmie.

Jacob and Violet had met, Susie learned, during the war while Jacob had been stationed at Fort Benning, Georgia. Violet left her Georgia home and family to return to these Pennsylvania hills with Jacob.

"She's very lonely," Susie told me at supper Tuesday evening. "She didn't say much, but I think Jacob must be pretty ugly when he's drinking." Susie smiled beguilingly. "I needed some sugar, dear, so I borrowed it from Violet. I must be sure to take it back."

Susie hiked back to the Petit home on Friday to return the sugar. Her report consisted of the familiar old story—a drinking husband, good and kind when sober, but quarrelsome and abusive when under the influence of alcohol.

"Can't you do something, Kenneth?" Susie chided. "You understand the problem well."

"I can't do anything but pray, dear," I replied. "Jacob keeps me at arm's length. He won't open up to me." And pray we did.

Our garden did well that year. Susie noticed that our neighbor's plot suffered much from neglect and produced little food. "I'm going to take Violet some of these nice, ripe tomatoes," she decided as we worked together preparing our vegetables for delivery in town one hot summer afternoon. "They haven't had any, I'm sure." She laid aside three round red fruits for the Petit family.

Evening arrived before she had opportunity to deliver the gift. Susie didn't linger long, which was unusual. Her breath came with deep gasps when she paused beside me at the well pump where I had stopped to relax for a moment. In the background Vernon noisily pushed the mower around and around the house, clipping the grass.

"Susie! Is anything wrong? Why did you rush so?"

Susie breathed deeply. "Violet and Jimmy are gone . . . back to Georgia," she gasped.

"Back to . . . Georgia? You mean . . ." I couldn't put it into words.

"Mr. Petit says they left him over a week ago," Susie reported. She dropped down on the well top beside me.

"Why did she go, Susie?"

"You know how he is when he's drinking," Susie answered. I nodded agreement. I remembered only too well my introduction to Jacob Petit.

"She threatened to leave sometime ago, but I didn't take it

seriously. I should have," Susie said remorsefully. "I don't believe I even prayed about it."

"Let's do that right now, Susie," I suggested. We experienced wonderful fellowship with the Lord around our outdoor altar, surrounded by the trees, garden plots, and singing birds. His presence soothed our troubled hearts.

God does answer prayer. Because of a severe cold, Susie did not accompany me to church on Sunday evening. I thought about Jacob—alone, unhappy, and probably drunk—as I approached his dark, silent house on my way home.

"Speak to Jacob!" The command exploded in my mind.

"But Lord, the house is dark!" I hedged, slowing the car to a crawl and checking the windows for light. I really didn't want to talk to Jacob. I was happy to remind the Lord that the house was dark, indicating that Jacob must be in bed, sleeping. I drove past the house, up the hill to my own lane, and Susie.

"Go and speak to Jacob!" The command returned emphatically.

"All right, Lord," I bargained. "I'll go back. If I see a light, I'll believe you've sent me to speak to Jacob."

I stopped at the house briefly to inform Susie of my whereabouts, and to ask her to pray for the success of my endeavor, should Jacob be up when I reversed my steps. As I faced the descent, the hillside below me breathed gloominess. Darkness shrouded the Petit house. I almost said, "See, Lord . . ." when a light suddenly appeared in the front room. My heart raced as I applied the brake and parked the vehicle.

The door opened beneath my knock.

"Good evening, Jacob."

"Good evening, Eagle. Won't you come in?" Jacob stepped back and motioned me inside.

"I drove by a few minutes ago and the house was dark," I said casually. Was the Lord *really* in this? I had to know. "How do you happen to be up now?"

Jacob looked at me. For once his curt rude manner was gone. His face revealed his unhappiness. Deep lines creased his forehead; dark circles shadowed his eyes. "I couldn't sleep, Mr. Eagle. For some reason I felt that I just had to get up. Why did you come back?"

I marvelled at the mighty hand of God. "The Lord sent me to talk to you—about Violet and Jimmy, Jacob," I replied. "I told Him if you had a light when I came back, I'd stop and talk to you. It was His Holy Spirit which moved you to get up, Jacob."

Jacob shook his head wonderingly. "Does He really care that

much?" he asked, scratching the toe of his shoe across the worn carpet.

"Yes, He does."

I talked to Jacob for over an hour. Together, we journeyed back to the days of my childhood in these hills, through the years of Dad's business venture and my own addiction to alcohol.

"Christ freed me from the snares of alcohol, Jacob. He can do the same for you," I encouraged. "Give your heart to Him; He'll help you to be a good husband and father."

"I'll think about it; truly—I will," Jacob promised, looking me squarely in the eyes.

"Will you at least agree to go to Georgia and bring your wife and son home, Jacob? They need you, and you need them," I urged, as we stood together inside the open door.

Tears glistened in my neighbor's eyes. "Yes," he nodded. "And I will be a better husband and father."

Jacob kept his word. Violet and Jimmy joined him in their house under the hill. However, twenty-five years later, we are still praying for Jacob's salvation.

XVIII

A WHITE SHIRT SPEAKS

The Lord issued no warning. Nothing about this dark, gloomy morning indicated its imminent chaotic effect upon my life, my hopes, my plans, yes, even my very outlook toward the future. It caught me completely by surprise.

"Would you take these kitchen scraps out for the geese, Kenneth?" Susie inquired Tuesday morning, November 15.

I accepted the pan of cabbage leaves and other assorted leftovers. Pausing at the door, I spoke to Vernon, who still sat at the breakfast table, "Are you about ready to help water the laying hens, Vernon?"

Vernon pushed his chair away from the table, and we stepped out together into a drenching fall downpour.

Noisily, the geese, all 70 of them, surrounded us as I flung the scraps onto the gravel driveway. We had found that town people willingly paid a fair price for dressed fowl, so we had added fat, plucked geese to our list of market products. They supplied a source of income during the winter months when we no longer had fresh garden produce to sell.

Back and forth through the rain we plodded, carrying heavy buckets of water to the chickens. A strange inner compulsion gripped me. "Go to the house!"

"But that's foolish!" I argued to myself. "I just came from the house and everything was all right then."

The feeling persisted. "Go to the house! Something is going on in there."

Fearing that perhaps Susie or Michael had been hurt, and that for some reason Susie could not call me, I dropped my buckets and hurried to the house.

The rain pounded fiercely against the metal roof of the house, subduing my entrance into the kitchen. Susie stood at the ironing board, laboring over my white dress shirt. Tears fell profusely. When she discovered my presence, she shook her head with exasperation and tried unsuccessfully to control her weeping.

"Susie! What are you crying about?" I asked with concern. I searched my mind for some clue to those tears. I remembered our conversation at breakfast. I had teased her about the lumpy cream of wheat. Perhaps I had injured her feelings with my careless talk.

"Did I hurt your feelings this morning when I teased you about the cereal?" I inquired.

"No," Susie replied, wiping her eyes with the tail of her apron, "you didn't hurt my feelings."

Thoroughly confused, I probed further. "Well, what is it then? What *did* I do?"

"You didn't do anything, dear."

"Susie, what *is* wrong? Did you burn yourself on the iron?"

Baffled, I slumped into a kitchen chair. My wife sniffed, wiped her eyes and shook her head negatively.

A new thought entered my mind. I knew Susie hated to iron white shirts, so I grasped at that clue.

"I know you don't like to iron white shirts, *but* I didn't know it was *that* bad," I ventured.

"I'm not weeping because I don't like to iron white shirts," my Susie replied. She stood the iron on end and faced me.

"Well," I demanded, impatiently, I'm afraid, "What is it then?"

Had I known what troubled my wife, I'm sure I wouldn't have asked, but I didn't know. And Susie in tears was a disturbing rarity!

"It's because God speaks to me while I'm ironing your white shirts."

"Oh, He does!" I marvelled. "What does He say to you?" I asked, wondering what God would have to say about white shirts. I didn't realize that He was speaking to my wife about me.

"Well," she replied reluctantly, "it isn't the shirts that He speaks to me about; it's you."

"What does He say?" If I had known what was coming, I certainly would not have pursued the subject, but curiosity caused me to blunder ahead.

"He tells me to iron them tenderly and lovingly because some day soon He's going to send you out into evangelistic work, and I'll have to pack them up." She added, with a catch in her voice, "And maybe sometimes months will go by before I'll see you."

Lightning striking couldn't have produced a greater upheaval. Stunned, bewildered, angry, I turned back into the pounding rain, dashed across the lawn and into the barn. I searched for a place of privacy. The haymow! The ladder squeaked protestingly as my 200 pounds touched each cross piece.

I sank to my knees in the fragrant clover. My fists clenched tightly in rebellion. I shook them in my Lord's face and said aloud, "Oh God, send somebody else. Don't send me; you know I love my home and my family. And I love my little chicken farm."

Nothing earth-shattering followed that heartfelt utterance. I meant that prayer. I didn't want to leave my wife and our small son. Working with chickens suited me fine; I had loved them ever since Dad had brought Biddy from Smith's years before. And I loved to eat them, especially fried.

And besides, weren't there other people better qualified than I to bring the gospel to others? "I'm just a hillbilly, Lord," I informed Him, as though He didn't know that. "Bootlegger Ralph's brat. Don't you remember?"

"A bootlegger, saved by grace," my Lord reminded me, gently and reproachfully.

The Lord also brought to my memory that wordless call experienced while I was still in school. At that time I had cried, "Lord, I know you're calling, but I don't know what you are calling me for. Just show me what you want me to do."

Could it be? Could the Lord be using Susie to show me the answer to that cry? Me, unlearned, uneducated—a man of the hills? Only once had I mentioned the unspoken call of my younger years to Susie. A sudden recollection of our experience in the raspberry patch made the happening of this day even more devastating. Could it be possible that the Lord was calling me to preach? I shook myself in rebellion.

Finally, I went back to the house. Susie placed baby Michael in his crib and turned to face me. That picture remains even yet, touchingly beautiful, in my memory. Placing her arms around my waist, with tears still falling, she looked into my face. Almost as if our former conversation had not been interrupted, she continued, "I want you to know that when that day does come, dear, I'll never stand in your way."

It must be human nature which causes us to resist those things that go against our wishes, even when we know that the thing we're resisting is God's will for us. Fortunately for us, God's mercy is boundless. He proceeded at once to bend my stubborn spirit.

XIX

WHOM THE LORD LOVETH . . .

God spoke to me through many means—our chicken farm, our family, and our neighbors.

I discovered to my horror one January day following Mother's death in August, that Dad had trucked all of our familiar household furniture to a central auction house where it had been knocked off to the highest bidder. I'm sure he thought the material things of our old home were of little value, and that was true with the exception of the old family Bible. It had been packed in an old trunk and forgotten.

Frankly, I was shocked. In vain I tried to locate the buyer, but no one seemed to know where it had gone. Losing that Bible was like losing a beloved member of the family all over again. I had hoped that it would one day occupy the place of honor in our home. Now, it was gone.

That Bible haunted me. It had been such a blessing in our home as I was growing up. Where was it now? Was it serving a similar function in the home to which it had gone? Or, had its purchaser bought it merely as an ornament, to be looked at on the outside but not to be loved and used? Would I ever know? I found myself praying that this precious book might serve as a means of spiritual growth in the home to which it had gone.

The arrival of our baby girl, Joyce, forced my mind from trivial matters to those of greater importance. Due to a blizzard which descended from the north blocking the road, three days passed before I could see her. Only after neighbors opened the roads and took down fences could I get through to the hospital to visit my wife and baby daughter.

Our little girl thrilled us. From the first Susie had hoped for a black-eyed baby daughter. Our Heavenly Father graciously granted her desire. Her eyes were as black as coal. Very happy, we took our little one home to join Michael, Ellen, and Vernon.

Dad dropped over one day in mid March. "Aunt Mabel died last night; she will be buried Thursday afternoon," he informed us sadly.

With a sudden prick of fear, Aunt Mabel's words, uttered at the time of Mother's breakdown, returned to haunt me. During the years since that time, I had never been able to shake myself entirely free of them. "They'll all end up in the crazy house," Aunt Mabel had prophesied. I hadn't thought of those words for some months. Now they returned to plague me.

Susie and I, in our relatively new role as parents, weren't aware that we should not have taken Joyce out that cold windy day for the graveside committal service. She came down with a cold almost immediately.

Joyce cried incessantly. Her tiny hands clawed at the sides of her face until her cheeks were raw and bleeding. We knew something was wrong with the infant.

"This child has a very bad ear infection," the doctor informed us, giving us a prescription for medicine. "It should do the job. It if doesn't, bring her back." Our hopes high, we took our little one home again.

But the condition didn't get better. We took the child back to the doctor. He tried another type of medicine, hoping it would succeed in clearing up the infection. This effort met with failure.

"Let's try an ear specialist, dear," Susie suggested. "We can't go on like this."

And indeed, something had to be done. The infant slept very little during the night, and only by catnaps in the day. Both Susie and I felt the strain of those interrupted nights.

"I'll have to put this child in the hospital and operate on those ears," the specialist told us. "She'll be there several days." The operation seemed to be successful.

Three days later, and happier than we had been since this illness struck, we picked Joyce up at the hospital and started toward the hills.

"She looks wonderful, Kenneth," Susie rejoiced as we drove away from the city. "Isn't it a relief to have her well again?"

I nodded thankfully. "Yes, dear. It's worth all we have spent just to see our daughter looking so healthy."

Lightning struck from another source when I got home that afternoon.

"The chickens are dying, Kenneth," Vernon reported. True, Vernon's mind didn't function normally, but he knew if a chicken was dead or alive! When he told me the chickens were dying, I realized that something drastic must be wrong.

I couldn't tag the ailment that had hit our flocks. I called the poultry doctor, who came and examined them.

"You'll have to sell them at once, or you'll lose most of them," he told me honestly. "It's a new disease for which we have no cure at this time. Newcastle disease, we call it."

We sold the chickens. This loss robbed us of our chief source of income. I went back to work in the grocery store.

To add to our woes, Joyce began to cry and fret. Soon, instead of simple matter draining from her ears, a bloody flux oozed from each and down the side of her face. Desperately we prayed, hoping the Lord would hear us in our anguish and heal her.

We slept in shifts. Susie was as tired as I. I would sit by her crib and rock it back and forth, back and forth, until I had no more energy to do so. Susie would take my place, while I dropped exhausted into bed. Sometimes Joyce would close her eyes and we would tip toe hopefully to bed, only to have her draw up in pain, scream, and claw at her ears. Susie or I would get up and rock the crib again in a vain attempt to lull the infant to sleep.

The doctors seemed to be helpless. We took her to one, then another, borrowing money to pay each one his required fee for services rendered.

"I wonder if Dad could help us, Susie?" I mused one day. "After all, Vernon and Ellen are really his responsibility. I think I'll ask him."

Since Mother's death, Dad's shoulders had slumped. He moved in a daze. I hated to worry him with our problems but felt I had no choice.

"Dad, we've got more than our share of responsibility," I began. "We're going deeper into debt all the time with the mortgage on the place, having to sell the chickens and this illness of the baby's. If you could give us a little support for Vernon . . ."

"I'm sorry, Kenneth," Dad interrupted, "but I barely earn enough to feed and clothe myself. I'm afraid Vernon is your headache now."

And that was that.

We prayed earnestly that God would show us a solution to our financial woes.

I almost dreaded coming home in early afternoon. It meant arriving to find a crying, fretful baby and a tired, dispirited wife. My own discouragement added nothing to the atmosphere of our home. Driving up the hill in a dreary mood one afternoon, I barely noticed the moving truck in front of the Petit home and the "For Sale" sign in the yard as I passed the house.

"Violet was up to say good-bye today," Susie said sadly as she rocked the baby and fed her formula. She eyed the bottle critically. "Kenneth, I'm worried. Joyce doesn't drink nearly as much as she should . . ."

"I don't know what more we can do, Susie," I replied with tears in my eyes and voice. "We've prayed fervently for her recovery; we've taken her to all the doctors we know of . . ."

"I know, dear," my wife answered gently.

That evening I tried, as I always did, to read my Bible before retiring. Mark 16 happened to be on my schedule. The second section of verse 18 hit me like a ton of brick. "They shall lay hands on the sick, and they shall recover."

"Surely you don't mean that I'm to lay my hands upon Joyce, Lord!" I sputtered. "That command was just meant for the apostles, wasn't it? It's not supposed to apply to *our* day, is it?" And so I silenced that little whisper that said, "Lay hands upon the child and pray for her in the name of the Lord Jesus."

The answer to our financial dilemma developed slowly, but snowballed, once it dawned in our minds.

"If we didn't have such large mortgage payments to meet, we'd manage a lot better," I mused to Susie.

Suddenly, Susie's eyes opened wide. "Kenneth! It's so obvious! Why don't we sell this place and buy the Petit place? It's much smaller. The mortgage on it won't be nearly so hard to meet."

"Sell *this* place, Susie? Sell our home, our little chicken farm, and our truck gardens? Do you mean it?" I must have sounded somewhat shocked.

Susie nodded soberly. "I think the Lord has been trying to show us that, Kenneth. Have you forgotten what happened to the chickens?" She paused while my cheeks, I fear, reddened. "And the Petit place is for sale. I think this is the Lord's will for us."

My wife considered a moment, while I remained rebelliously silent. "Why don't we move ahead slowly, on the premise that this is the Lord's will, and if nothing hinders, we can be sure of it?"

Unwillingly, I agreed. I still loved that little chicken farm, and wasn't ready to part with it. However, developing events hastened, rather than impeded, that action.

XX

TESTING

We listed our home with a realtor, then investigated the possibility of purchasing the Petit place. We found it to our liking, but another crisis erupted before a buyer appeared for our property.

Mark 16:18 continued to haunt me. I couldn't get away from it. I thought about it constantly. Finally, without telling Susie of my plans, I took time off during my lunch hour at the grocery and went to talk it over with Albert Lightfoot.

"Brother Albert, was this verse," I pointed to the passage, "meant to apply only to the apostles, or does it carry over to us?"

The older man studied the verse thoughtfully. "I've always thought it applied to the apostles, Kenneth. I've never heard of anyone who practiced it in our times. Have you?"

I had to acknowledge that I had not.

"Why do you ask?" Brother Albert wondered.

"Our baby girl has been ill with an ear infection for almost six months," I replied tearfully. "The doctors seem to be helpless. We've prayed, but . . ."

"We'll be praying for her, too, son," Brother Lightfoot encouraged, placing a sympathetic arm around my shoulders. Curiously let down, I thanked him and returned to the store.

It happened to be Susie's turn to stay with Joyce on Sunday, since taking her to church was impossible. I had been elected Sunday School superintendent the previous year; Joyce's illness had placed my duties on an alternating basis with my assistant, John Ramer.

"She's no better?" John asked with concern that Sunday in October when I entered the building alone except for Ellen and Vernon.

"No better," I replied with sagging shoulders.

"Why don't you take her to Dr. Green in Allentown? My brother had a bad ear infection and he cleared it up quickly," John suggested. "I've heard other people say that he is very good, too."

"Thank you, John. This may be the answer to our prayers," I replied, gripping his hand firmly in gratitude.

We made the thirty-mile trip to Allentown on Tuesday. Together, Susie and I walked into Dr. Green's office, carrying the little girl. He invited us to be seated, took one look at his patient and said, "Why did you wait so long to bring her? Why didn't you bring her sooner?"

His questions hurt deeply. We had done everything we could for the child, and had we known of his reputation we would have brought her to him before. In my anguish, I attempted to explain this to Dr. Green. He nodded understandingly and continued his examination.

"Among other things," the doctor said at last, "your daughter is anemic. And if she lives," we froze in our chairs and Susie's face blanched, "she probably will be a deaf mute because she is so very young." He looked at our stricken faces and added, "Also, since she probably won't be able to hear, she also will not learn to speak."

He paused a moment, considering our black-eyed, black-haired baby. "I'm committing her to the hospital. We'll put her on penicillin and see what happens, but I'm not too hopeful." He called the Allentown General Hospital and made the arrangements. With leaden hearts Susie and I carried the infant into the building to her ward.

"I'm going to be brave," I said to myself as I turned to leave the room. But as the door closed behind us, the thought that this might be the last time we would see our daughter alive, tormented me. Right there in that long hospital corridor I turned to Susie, and we wept in each other's arms.

That night we turned Joyce completely over to the Lord. Susie rose from her knees rejoicing. "Praise the Lord! I'm so happy!" she exclaimed.

"Happy? With our little girl in the hospital at the point of death?" I'm sure my voice reeked with incredulity.

Susie's face radiated joy. "Yes. I'm still happy in spite of that. I'm happy in the Lord. I rejoice, even if we never see her again, that the Lord gave us the joy of looking into her face and of having her in our home these few months."

My wife's happiness proved contagious. Soon I too was rejoicing and praising the Lord for giving us this child, even though He might take her from us.

However, an immediate problem faced us—hospital and doctor bills. We turned to the Lord for help.

Almost at once a buyer appeared for our place and we found ourselves financially able to purchase the Petit place. Although we still carried a mortgage, it was much smaller, and we were able to channel more funds into the accumulating bills.

We executed the move while Joyce was in the hospital.

"If we wait until she is home, Kenneth, it may be quite some time before we can move," my wife reasoned. "She'll not be strong yet . . ."

And her reasoning proved sound. "She isn't quite what she should be yet," Dr. Green said, after two weeks had elapsed, "but she needs a mother's care and love. I'm releasing her tomorrow."

Our '32 Chevie lacked a heater so we borrowed the money and installed one before we picked the infant up at the hospital. With high hopes we deposited Joyce in her own crib in our new home.

Would this nightmare never end? No sooner had we gotten the child home than the trouble began all over again: the bloody flux draining from her ears, the screaming, the crying, the writhing and twisting in pain. In addition, she refused to take enough nourishment. We feared the anemia would return.

We prayed, begging the Lord to hear us and deliver us from our plight. The child's condition continued to deteriorate.

I arrived home on Thursday evening to find Susie in tears. The doctor had seen Joyce that day. ". . . and if this continues, she'll have to go back to the hospital," my wife reported. "She has a badly congested chest."

Even then I could hear that wee bundle of flesh wheezing and wheezing. Her food refused to stay down. Weakly, she retched, but hardly seemed strong enough to bring the food up.

With a sick feeling in the pit of my stomach, I went to work on Friday morning. During the course of the day, Sadie Brown stopped in to make a purchase.

"Brother Eagle! How are you this morning?"

"I'm happy in the Lord but . . ." I knew Sister Brown as a devout Christian lady, although she was not a member of my denomination, so I told her about our baby girl and her illness.

Sadie Brown looked directly into my eyes and asked, "Haven't you prayed for her?"

Flabbergasted, I replied, "Certainly, Sister Brown, we've prayed for her."

She watched me closely as she asked, "But have you prayed for her according to Mark 16:18, *with the laying on of the hands?*"

That question struck me right between the eyes.

"But wasn't that for the apostles, Sister Brown?" I asked. I added, "I've had the conviction to do this, Sister. I even talked to Brother Lightfoot about it. He felt it belonged to apostolic days. I stifled my convictions."

Sister Brown replied firmly, words that have stayed with me and helped me find my way many times in doubtful situations, "Remember this, young man; convictions will never do you any good unless they are carried out and acted upon." The Lord had shown me the answer to our daughter's desperate illness. Did I have the faith to carry it out? And the courage?

When I reached home late that night, it had been my long day at the store, I opened the door to see baby Joyce in her crib by the stove, wheezing, crying, and gasping for breath. Her whimper was so faint and hoarse I could hardly hear it. Susie lay on the couch nearby, crying silently.

"Mother, what is wrong?" I asked.

"I'm afraid she'll have to go back to the hospital tomorrow. The doctor thinks she might be getting pneumonia," Susie cried.

I got ready for bed. Conviction burned deep within me, but I silenced it, afraid to share with anyone, even my wife. Suddenly, it came to me so significantly. What would the results be if I *refused* to obey what the Lord had clearly shown me to be *His* will? Could I expect healing for my child from some other source if I rejected the way He had revealed to me?

I turned on the light, picked up my Bible and found Mark 16. I read aloud, "And these signs shall follow those that believe . . . they shall lay hands on the sick, and they shall recover."

"Susie, do you believe that?"

My wife literally leaped from the bed and said, "I believe it with all my heart."

We brought the child and laid her on the studio couch where we had been sleeping. Together, we placed our hands upon her head and prayed in the name of Jesus.

The miracle happened! Immediately the crying stopped; the wheezing, gasping breathing subsided into the sweet regular breathing of a well child. She fell asleep. Susie and I stared at one another in amazement. We wept and we laughed; we rejoiced and praised the Lord together. Then, because it was only through His mercy that her life had been spared, we dedicated this child to the God of Heaven.

That Sunday, for the first time in five months, we attended church together.

"What happened to your baby?" friends asked. We told them the story. Many rejoiced with us, but there were some who laughed in derision.

The Lord's healing has been complete. As time passed, no impediment in speech or hearing hindered the normal development of our child. In fact, I sometimes think she hears a little better than she should!

As I look back across the accumulation of almost a quarter of a century, and the events that crowd into part of a lifetime, I never realized then that same little bundle of possibilities, our Joyce, would one day become the bride of Brother Allen Martz's youngest son. Nor did it enter my mind that at this very moment they would be preparing to bring the light of the Gospel to one of the far corners of our dark world, she as a registered nurse, and he as a co-pilot of God.

My world seemed to be settling back to normal. The announcement that a slate for the ordination of a deacon at Oberlin would be taken in two weeks didn't concern me too much. After all, hadn't the white shirt said I was to *preach?*

XXI

ONLY A DEACON . . .

"Dear, we really ought to be giving more of our time to the Lord's work," Susie chided on that lovely October morning as we sat at the breakfast table.

"We can't, dear," I replied, sensibly, I thought. "Don't you recall the unpaid hospital bill, and my inheritance from Father?" My only "inheritance" from Father had been Vernon. To meet the remaining bills following Joyce's illness, I had shouldered another job—cleaning chickens in a poultry processing plant. In order to save transportation money, I had also purchased a used motor scooter.

"Yes, I'm remembering the bills and your "inheritance" from Father," Susie replied quietly. "But God has promised to supply our needs, Kenneth, if we put Him first . . ."

"If He wants me in full-time service, won't He show me that, Mother?" I asked stubbornly. I really wasn't interested in full-time service; I was dodging the issue and Susie knew it.

"He'll tell you if you'll let Him," my wife replied soberly.

My name in the lot for deacon jolted me from my apathy. "But Susie . . ." I fretted.

Susie read my thoughts. "I know, Kenneth. Your primary mission will be evangelism, but you're not ready to preach yet." She paused consideringly. "Perhaps," she continued, "the Lord plans to use this position as deacon as preparation for the larger task. If the Lord does place you in this office, use it to foster spiritual growth and maturity."

The lot of deacon fell to me. Ordination took place on October 15, 1947.

I followed Susie's wise counsel and began carrying my Bible to work daily. During my lunch hour I hopped on the scooter and rode to my outdoor woodland cathedral under the trees and there studied that ever more wonderful Book. Precious new truth sprang from its pages as I pored over them day after day.

But my Lord now undertook another step in my education. The telephone rang one evening sometime later.

"It's Brother Miller, over at Milltown, dear," Susie informed me, handing me the receiver.

After the formalities had been dispensed with, Brother Miller asked, "Would you consider preaching for us Sunday, Brother Eagle? Brother Jones is ill and we just can't find anyone."

"I'm not a minister, Joe," I replied evasively. "I'm only a deacon."

"I'm aware of that, but deacons are authorized to preach when no minister is available, are they not?" Brother Joe returned quickly from his end of the line.

I hedged. "Let me talk to Bishop Howard about it first, Joe," I answered. "I'll call you back later."

Susie glanced at me questioningly as I replaced the telephone. "He wants me to preach at Milltown Sunday," I reported shortly.

"Some of the deacons in the early church *did* preach," Susie reminded me. "Stephen and Philip did. Remember?"

"I know," I replied miserably. "I guess I just don't want to preach."

"Dear," Susie replied, laying aside her dishcloth and coming to stand with her arms around my ample waist, "don't stand in the way of the Lord's blessing in your life. Stop fighting His will for you. Call Brother Howard," she urged. "If he agrees, you can accept with confidence any calls to preach that come to you."

I heaved a vast sigh of resignation. "All right, Susie. If the Lord wants me to preach Sunday, I'll preach."

That preaching appointment led to others. One cool rainy Sunday I had been asked to speak at Bluebelle, a small hill church about thirty miles away. I decided to ride the scooter, since this would free the car for Susie and the children. I had forgotten that the gas gauge had conked out the previous week. It registered half-full when I donned rain coat, poncho and rubbers and headed out of the hills across the valley.

I had almost reached my destination when the scooter sputtered and stopped. The gas gauge still reported the tank to be half-filled. I remembered suddenly that the gauge didn't work. After taking stock of my predicament, I thanked the Lord for His goodness. My vehicle had halted only one hundred yards from the home of Art Good, a cousin of Susie's. In front of his garage stood a gas pump!

Art cheerfully filled my gas tank. "Here, Art; let me pay you for the gas," I said, removing my billfold.

Art shook his head negatively. "No, Kenneth. You're a servant of the Lord and engaged in His work. I'm giving the gas to Him."

I couldn't argue with that philosophy. "Thank you, Art," I replied, and proceeded to my appointment.

Following that service the rain had ceased. I stuffed my wet-weathered gear in the saddle bags on the scooter and prepared to take off. The Sunday school superintendent stood beside me. His pre-occupied manner told me that something bothered him. I waited.

"Brother Eagle, doesn't it seem a bit out of place to you for a minister to arrive at church riding a motor scooter?" he asked bluntly.

That question put me on the spot! As I cast about in my mind for a convincing answer, the Lord came to my rescue through Joe Miller.

"Wouldn't you rather see him come riding a scooter, Brother, rather than driving a big Buick or a Cadillac?" he asked mildly.

My critic grinned broadly. "I would, at that," he acknowledged. "I hadn't thought of it that way." He shook my hand warmly, and I departed for home on my noisy conveyance.

This speaking engagement led to an invitation to hold revival meetings in that church. I felt I could not do this, and our bishop brethren concurred. I refused the invitation.

However, these preaching assignments opened my eyes to the need for a deeper knowledge of the Word of God. "I wish I could attend Bible School somewhere," I told Susie.

"Ask, and it shall be given you," Susie reminded me with a smile. We began praying about the matter, and the Lord opened the door to a period of Bible study at a school in Kitchener, Ontario, Canada. That was my first acquaintance with Ontario. It seems strange now, when I've spent so many happy times in that province, that I had no inkling then of the place it would fill in my life.

An invitation of another sort surprised us in the summer of 1950. Allen Martz and I had kept in touch over the years through an occasional letter or card. A letter arrived inviting me to come to Minnesota to teach Bible school among the Indians with whom Allen and Betsy were working.

"What shall I say, Susie?"

"Let's pray about it, Kenneth," she suggested.

Susie talked as she went about placing supper on the table. "Sally Lightfoot is bedridden now, Kenneth," she said quietly. "Brother Albert would like for us to call on Mrs. Jenkins over at Bluebelle. She is desperately ill."

I thought about that request from my dear friend, Albert Lightfoot. Where would I be now, had it not been for this dear and devoted layman? What would have been my fate, had he not taken the time to visit us many years before? I made a quick decision.

"Of course we'll go, Susie. Would it suit you this evening? Tomorrow is my long day again," I reminded her.

"Yes, I can make it suit tonight," she answered. "Oh, Kenneth! I just wish we could take over the visiting for Brother Albert. With Sister Sally so ill . . ."

"I know, Susie. It's a shame we can't do more of the visiting, but with two jobs to take care of . . ."

"Aren't the hospital bills about paid now, dear?" Susie asked, pouring tea into glasses on the table. "Do you really need to keep the job at the poultry plant?"

"How'd she know?" I speculated silently. I replied audibly, "This week's pay will finish them up."

"Wonderful!" Susie's eyes sparkled. "Then we can do more visiting, can't we?" she asked hopefully.

"We'll see how everything works out," I said.

We went to see Mrs. Jenkins and had the pleasure of sharing spiritually with her. That visit crystallized Susie's determination to do more of this type of work.

We had prayed much about the invitation from Allen Martz. "I think you should go," Susie encouraged. "Fellowshipping with Allen will be good for you. And getting a broader view of the Lord's vineyard will enlarge your vision."

I sensed an "at homeness" among those Indian people. They struggled with the same poverty and sins which had plagued my home when I was a boy. I longed, in some way, to reach out and open the eyes of these spiritually blind, to free them from the snares of the evil one. Strangely, after many years, I began to glimpse the direction in which the Lord's will for me lay.

If this Bible school assignment permitted me a *glimpse* of what the future held, I hardly knew how to describe the Lord's next revelation!

With the call of the Lord heavy on my heart, I went to work at the poultry plant one afternoon following my return from Minnesota. As we worked at the eviscerating table, a sister in our church who stood at the opposite side of the table from me suddenly dropped her knife and burst into tears. I thought she had cut her finger.

"Ruth! What happened? Are you hurt?"

I don't believe lightning striking could have stunned me more than her reply.

"Brother Eagle, evangelize!"

"What?" I fumbled for words, wondering if I had understood correctly. "What did you say, Ruth?"

"The Lord told me to tell you to evangelize," she answered, wiping her tears. "He has more than chickens in life for you!"

Immediately my mind raced back to the time a few years back when I had shaken my fist in my Lord's face and asked Him not to give me this type of work. I had told Him that I loved my little chicken farm. I realized bleakly that drastic measures had been necessary to free me from its grip. Shaken to my very soul, I hastened to the rest room and fell prostrate to the floor and wept before my God. "Father, if this be Thy will, please show me and make a way so that I can carry it out."

Lightning can strike twice in the same place, I assure you! The next day, at almost the same hour of the day, Eva Downs, a Brethren lady, dropped her knife and burst into tears.

"Eva, is something wrong? Are you hurt?"

"Brother Eagle, you must evangelize! The Lord told me to tell you to preach the Gospel!" she replied, wiping her tears.

My thought jumped to Ruth. Those were almost her exact words. "Have you been talking to Ruth?" I demanded.

"Oh, no! The Lord told me to tell you. Why did you ask that?"

"She told me almost exactly the same thing yesterday," I replied, thoroughly shaken.

I needed no more evidence to convince me of the call of God, and of His will for my life. This time as I returned to the rest room and dropped to the floor, I yielded to the Lord. "Lord, if this is what you want me to do, I'm willing to follow. Only you must make a way financially for us."

One final event capped that decision and sealed our commitment.

XXII

THE GREAT SUPPLIER

The straw that broke the camel's back awaited me when I arrived home that memorable evening. It came in the form of a letter from Mrs. Jenkins, the sick lady whom Susie and I had visited earlier in the week. She thanked us for coming to see her and closed with the words, "May the Lord bless you and help you to give more of your time in the Lord's work."

I told Susie of my experience that day, and of my decision. We took the letter, and, as Hezekiah of old had done, we spread it out before the Lord. We talked the entire problem over with Him.

"Lord, you know we would like to give more of our time to your service. But Lord, here is our family—Vernon, Ellen, Michael, and Joyce, besides Susie and myself—and they all need food and clothing and a warm place to live." I paused, took a deep breath, and exercised my faith which at that moment seemed but as a grain of mustard seed, then went on. "Lord, if you'll provide financially for us and for my family, we'll give more of our time in your service."

That vow of commitment took place on Friday evening. We determined to begin our new schedule the next week.

"I'll start by dropping the job at the poultry plant," I decided, easing into a chair. Joyce trotted happily around the house, black curls bouncing. Eight-year-old Michael rode a broomstick horse across the floor. Vernon and Ellen sat at the table, each with a book. My heart rejoiced in my loved ones.

"You ought to speak to Mr. Myers at the grocery, Daddy," Susie encouraged. "You may need time off for emergency visitation." Her eyes followed mine as the children romped about. Her lips smiled tranquilly as she said, again sensing my thoughts, "Dear, you've trusted the Lord for your eternal salvation. Is it too much to trust Him to supply our physical needs as well?"

"You're right, Mother," I acknowledged. "I'll talk it over with Mr. Myers the first opportunity I have on Monday morning."

I guess Satan tries to make things look as difficult as he can to keep us from fully obeying the Lord. Talking to Web Myers wasn't half as bad as I had anticipated.

"Of course, Kenneth," he said heartily. "Take off as much time as you like. The Lord's work comes first." He opened a carton of coffee cans and stacked them on the shelf.

I warned, "I may have to take several days a week sometimes, sir."

"That's all right, Kenneth," he said, removing the last can from the box. "If you want to work for me only one day a week, you can." He added thoughtfully, "I wish more deacons were willing to share the responsibilities, and ease the work loads of their ministers and lay leaders."

That day's mail contained an exhilarating letter from Allen Martz. The Lord had opened the door to missions among the Indians living in islands scattered over a wide area in Lake-of-the-Woods, a large body of water lying between the United States and Canada, but largely in Canada.

Allen wrote, "Our Heavenly Father wonderfully provided us with a houseboat in which to live and several smaller boats (to be used in getting to the islands). It was necessary to get camping equipment, dehydrated food, life preservers, and other essential materials. Several weeks were spent in repairing the motor, painting and reconditioning the houseboat. How our hearts rejoiced when on July 7 we were able to sail down the Rainey River to the Lake-of-the-Woods to begin our work!"

The letter continued, telling of sailing conditions, rough water, and of difficulties in following the channel on the map. My heart almost stood still with Allen's as he told of being lost one day in one of the small boats for eight hours without food or supplies. He knew he must go west to reach the houseboat, but between which islands? Which waterway would be the channel, or which one would turn out a dead end after several miles of rowing? An Indian who knew the location of the houseboat directed him back to it.

Brother Allen listed his fellow workers as Jimmie Byler and Elsie Reinbold, names which meant nothing to me. Jimmie, he stated was a young man from the east, and Elsie a converted Norwegian from his congregation in Minnesota. Betsy remained at home with the children.

Personally, I rejoiced that a strong chord of faith in the infallible and all powerful Heavenly Father sounded forth from every line. Although I never expected it to happen, my heart ached for the opportunity to share in this work of bringing the Gospel to these deprived people.

Even though these Indians were being reached with the good

news, Allen wasn't satisfied. His vision reached further. "Two hundred miles north of Kenora, Ontario, live large groups of Indians, mostly Chippewa and Cree. Very few of the Indians in this vast area are having the Gospel brought to them. Christ prayed for these souls in John 17. Let us fall on our knees and pray for the salvation of the souls in this area."

Brother Allen's letter encouraged me in my own decision to move ahead in the Lord's work.

Our first test came that week. Susie began using our car on Monday morning to transport children to Bible school. New tires for it had been one item I had relegated to the "will have to wait" list. We had no spare tire.

Monday evening we left the children with Ellen while Susie and I called upon a very sick sister near Oberlin. As we drove toward home, one of the tires blew out with a sickening lurch of the car.

"Oh, my!" Susie exclaimed.

"What do we do now?" I moaned. "We have no spare, dear."

After taking stock of our surroundings, Susie suggested, "Why don't you go over to that house and call John Miller?" She indicated a nearby dwelling.

It sounded like a good idea. I knocked at the door and introduced myself. "Good evening. I'm Kenneth Eagle. May I use your telephone?"

The homeowner graciously invited me in and showed me to the telephone. However, Brother John wasn't at home, and our dilemma remained unsolved. What should I do next?

"What is your problem, Mr. Eagle?" my host asked.

"I blew out a tire and have no spare," I replied.

"Don't worry about that, sir," my new friend said quickly. "I'm a garageman. I've a set of tires that will fit your car that I'll be glad to loan you." This fine gentleman went right out and put his tires on our car, and we drove home.

Susie drove the car to Bible school. I drove it to the store for groceries. We used it for visitation. It still carried the borrowed tires on its wheels.

"Susie," I protested, "we can't use this man's tires forever. We've got to do something."

My wife agreed that new tires had to come from somewhere. Finally, we borrowed the children's missionary money and went to John Miller, who loaned us enough to complete the purchase.

Although we had new tires on the car, and had returned those kindly loaned to us, I felt let down. We had told the Lord of our need, but He hadn't come through.

God is faithful, although we sometimes lose faith! On Thursday, a minister from a neighboring congregation called on us at our home. Before leaving, he placed a check on the table. "I want to give you this, Brother Eagle," he said. "I ought to spend more time in the Lord's work, but I don't."

The size of the check staggered me. "No, no, no, Brother!" I protested.

"Yes, yes, yes!" Susie interrupted. "This is the Lord's way." And truly it was His way. That check exactly covered the loan from John Miller and the money we had borrowed from the children. How we praised the Lord!

However, I now had only one dollar to my name. On Friday morning Susie said, "Oh, Daddy, we need some groceries."

"I know, Mother, but I have only $1.00," I replied.

Susie smiled. "Well, we promised the Lord we'd trust Him. The groceries can wait until next week," she decided, and immediately began planning on ways to stretch our meager larder.

We attended the Bible school program that evening. Just as we stepped from the lighted churchyard toward our car, a big automobile pulled up beside us. Friends from Philadelphia stepped out to greet us. They were returning to the city and just "happened" to see us. "The Lord told me to give you this," the brother said, handing me a ten-dollar bill. The Lord had known of our need and supplied it abundantly.

Michael's legs stuck out like toothpicks from his trousers. "Our son needs new trousers, Daddy," Susie remarked, pointing to that unsightly gap between pants and shoe tops.

"I know, Mother, but I don't have the money this week. Can you wait until next week?"

Patiently, my wife said, "Yes, we'll wait."

However, in our family devotions each evening, Susie faithfully reminded the Lord of this little boy's need of new trousers.

One day Mrs. Fox called Susie. "Come over to my house," she said. "I have some things for your sewing circle ladies."

When Susie told me of the call at the supper table that evening, I almost rebelled. "I've a notion not to go, Mother. You know how that last bunch of stuff was that she gave you—all dirty and tattered, almost useless. Why," I reinforced my argument, "didn't the sisters tell you not to bring any more things from her because it was too time consuming to go through for no more good than it was worth?" I set my water glass down carefully.

"Yes," Susie acknowledged. "They did say that. But let's not disappoint her, Daddy. Let's at least go and get the things. We can use the clothes for wipe-up rags, if they aren't fit for anything else."

When I arrived at her home, Mrs. Fox was her usual careless self. Her hair straggled uncombed about her face. Her dress needed mending in several places, and her general appearance would have profited from a generous application of soap and water.

She took me out to the hen coop. There, strewn across the floor were several articles of clothing. A number of pieces sprawled from a burlap sack tossed haphazardly across the water bucket.

Mr. Fox stuffed the garments, chicken filth and all, into the burlap bag and handed it to me, saying, "There you are, Mr. Eagle. If there is anything in there that your family can use, feel free to take it."

"Well!" I thought to myself, "there's nothing here we can use." Little did I know!

That evening my wife and the sewing circle sisters sorted through the bag of clothing. "Why, it's nothing but filthy rags!" they cried, emptying item after item from the sack. But Ada Miller paused as she came to the very bottom of the bag.

"What's this?" she exclaimed. She drew the garment out wonderingly. "Why, it's a little boy's suit! It looks practically new." She examined it carefully. "This seam is ripped," she reported, pointing to the pants leg, "but that is all I find wrong with it." Mrs. Miller sized up that suit and smiled at Michael. "Brother Eagle," she declared, "I believe this suit would fit your son."

Susie fixed the suit and we had it cleaned. Michael wore it to church and people said, "Oh, your son has a new suit!" I said, "Oh, no! He got that out of a rag bag." They could hardly believe it.

When Michael outgrew this fine suit, he passed it along to another boy in the congregation, who handed it down to his brother after he had outgrown it.

We praised the Lord for answered prayer. Immediately the Enemy challenged, "Oh, God will supply your need for a month, or perhaps a year. You'd better not expect too much. After all, you're still Bootlegger Ralph's brat!"

But, praise the Lord! Elijah's God is the same today and answers prayer in the same old way. And God's ravens are still in business.

We had only tapped the surface of His resources.

XXIII

PROPHECY FULFILLED

"Workers are desperately needed at Bluebelle Mission," Bishop Howard said to Susie and me one Sunday at Oberlin. "Would you consider accepting this assignment?"

We prayed over it. Consequently we began driving the thirty miles to Bluebelle every Sunday morning. Frequently I not only taught the youth class, but preached the sermon as well.

As the work grew, the bishop brethren decided, "We need a full-time pastor at Bluebelle." The brethren selected a date at which time a vote would be taken among the congregation for their choice of pastor.

Although I felt that the election would fall to me, I carried in my heart a deep burden. What did the future hold? Where would this step lead? Had my preparation been thorough enough? Could the Lord effectively use an uncultured individual such as I? After all, I was still "Bootlegger Ralph's brat," the Devil taunted. With these questions weighing my spirit I rode the scooter from the store at noon on the day of the ordination, to meditate in my forest cathedral.

Leaden clouds hung low; damp, gloomy mist filled the air. For the time being the rain had ceased. I entered the semi-circle of trees that formed the "cathedral" and knelt to pray. I committed my life anew to the Lord and asked that His will be done concerning the ordination.

Miraculously, an indescribable ray of light beamed from the dull grey skies, down through the trees and bathed my entire body in its light. I knelt there in timeless peace; then quite suddenly the light disappeared and the rain began again. It rained, and rained, and rained.

"It must have been the Lord's way of confirming your conviction of His call," Susie surmised when I shared the experience with her.

"That was my feeling, dear."

And the election did fall to me. I was ordained in 1952 and took over the pastorate of Bluebelle Mission.

Another blessing arrived in our home that same year—our second son, Luke Andrew Eagle.

Closely following my ordination came an invitation from

James Thacker to hold a series of revival meetings at Onion Run, Kentucky. He did not minimize the difficulty of the task, "Very few revivals have been held in this community," he wrote, "and the boys will probably try to whip you out and run you off. But will you come?"

Upon reading that letter my wife turned slightly pale. "I must go, Susie," I stated. "Those boys remind me so much of the kind of lad I was before Brother Albert came to us with the Gospel. I must try to reach them." Susie understood. "I'll be praying with all my heart," she promised.

On the evening before I departed for Onion Run, my wife prepared my favorite dish, fried chicken. Following the meal we all gathered in the living room where we read the Word and had special prayer together—prayer for the one who was leaving, and also for the ones who would be left behind. Then Susie and the family took me to the train. My wife sent me off to the Lord's work with a smile.

I will have to acknowledge that tears filled my eyes as the train rounded a bend and my loved ones vanished from sight. I had meant it when I told the Lord that I didn't want to go, and I wondered if, inside, perhaps, Susie was crying, too.

Once I had arrived in the hills of Kentucky, I had little time for homesickness. Bible school and revivals were being conducted jointly, Bible school in the morning and preaching in the evening. I shared a room in the Thacker home with Bud Green, a nineteen-year-old Bible school teacher.

"There have been only a few revivals in this area, as I mentioned in my letter," Brother Thacker informed me as we stopped by the "church" on the afternoon of my arrival. That structure happened to be an abandoned school building. We walked inside. Loose clapboards permitted sunlight to enter at many places, and also allowed free air circulation in addition to what came through the paneless windows.

I stood behind the teacher's desk and tried to imagine the congregation I might face. Brother Thacker's voice barged into my thoughts. "The boys are liable to poke you with sharp sticks through these holes, Brother Eagle," he warned, "so be ready for them." He pointed to the wall back of where I stood. Sunlight filtered through a crack where the clapboard was missing. People on the outside could easily jab the speaker on the inside, if they so wished. "They're determined to break up these meetings," Brother Thacker reported.

"I'll try to remember about the sticks," I promised.

But, I'm sorry to say, I didn't remember. That first evening as

I was speaking, emphasizing a high point in my sermon, I unexpectedly felt a sharp pain in my back. I jumped and yelled, and that was exactly what those boys wanted. They laughed and laughed. There must have been twenty boys between sixteen and eighteen years of age outside that building, all set to run this one poor preacher out of the country.

I prayed for help. Next time they jabbed me, I was ready. "Hallelujah!" I yelled. "The more you poke me, the louder I'll shout." That put an end to that kind of fun.

But we didn't know what to expect next. We didn't need to wonder long. The next evening the boys set fire to burlap bags and pitched them in the windows. Some of the brethren stomped out the flames. Even when not engaged in active harassment, the very presence of the boys outside the building proved distracting to those who were inside. I realized the battle had only begun. We were indeed in enemy territory.

Some of the older people declared that they were sorry about the disturbances, but Onion Run was too far from town or they'd ask the sheriff to arrest the youths. No help could be expected from that quarter. Someone would have to come up with another solution to the problem. My God has proved His power many times. I knew He could solve this dilemma. I turned it all over to Him.

A surprise of another sort jarred my composure as Bud Green and I prepared for bed that evening.

"Have you met the witch yet?" Bud asked, removing a shoe and dropping it to the floor with a thud.

"Which witch?" I quipped, grinning broadly.

"You think I'm joking, don't you?" Bud demanded, untying the second shoe.

I did, indeed. "Does she ride a Cadillac or a broomstick?" I teased, removing my own shoes.

Bud's face sobered. "Brother Eagle, I'm not joking. There is a witch here in the community. When you see her, you'll recognize her."

I must confess that I thought the boy was exaggerating. I only half believed him.

Our tormentors let us off with mild disorders on Wednesday evening. As time for the service approached on Thursday night, the atmosphere in the old school building grew tense. Those boys were all set to chase me out. I was equally determined, by the power of God, to stay. The boys would probably make a decisive move tonight, and none of us could anticipate what it might be. I prayed fervently that in some way God would overrule to His glory in the whole business.

And, Praise the Lord, He did! Abruptly, after the congregation had gathered, one of the brethren walked to the front of that rustic old building and stood by the desk. He bowed his head reverently and said, "Heavenly Father, I ask that if it be Your will, You will cause it to rain. Cause it to rain so hard that those boys who are outside this building will have to come into this building." He returned to his seat and sat down. An electric silence followed his prayer. The service opened as usual with a song.

As Bud Green announced the second song, the rain began. It descended as if someone had turned on a huge faucet. It came down in torrents. The water rose in the road until the boys crawled under the building, which stood on stilts, to keep dry. I continued preaching, almost shouting to be heard above the pounding of the rain. The water outside inched higher and higher, until, like a bunch of whipped puppies, the boys were forced to come into the building. It sounds unbelievable, but I was there and I ought to know!

After the meeting, with the rain still pouring down beyond those flimsy walls, the same brother again walked to the front of the church. "Father," he prayed, "will you stop the rain so that these dear people can get home without getting wet." Almost immediately the rain ceased. All of the congregation, except our group which travelled via jeep, and one family who rode a mule, had walked to the service. Everyone reached home safely except for two foolish boys who stupidly fell in the creek. For the remainder of the revivals those boys came in and gave the message their reverent attention.

The next morning upon opening her door in response to a knock, Mrs. Thacker found an unusual visitor waiting beyond the entry. A woman of about sixty years, clad entirely in scarlet, stood there. Red dress, red boots, huge red earrings, and a red turban knotted over bleached hair, constituted her attire. A heavy coating of makeup distorted her facial features. I gaped in wonder.

"Is that the woman, the witch?" I asked Bud in a whisper.

"That is she," he replied. "That is Ginger."

"Come in, Ginger," Sister Thacker invited. Another neighbor who had dropped in earlier moved into a corner of the kitchen as the red-clad figure entered the room. As Ginger stepped closer to her, this neighbor cried, "Go away, you old witch! Leave me alone. I haven't done anything to you!"

Something had to be done at once to ease the tense

atmosphere. I began to sing, "If you want joy, let Jesus come into your heart." Everyone joined in.

"I wish I could sing that and really mean it," Ginger said wistfully.

"You can, Ginger," Mrs. Thacker said lovingly. "Come over to the meetings tonight and find out how you can have real joy and peace. Will you?"

Ginger shook her head doubtfully. The mood had passed; she didn't want to talk anymore about spiritual things, and, for the time being, the Enemy had won another victory.

"Can I borrow a loaf of bread?" she asked.

"Surely."

The disreputable figure made its way down the road to a small house directly across the road from the school house and vanished inside. The neighbor sighed with relief.

"Why do you let her come here?" she demanded of Mrs. Thacker. "Aren't you afraid of her? She casts spells!"

Sister Thacker replied compassionately, "She needs the Lord Jesus just as badly as anyone else. He loves her, too." She added confidently, "We're not afraid. The power of Satan is nothing compared to the power of God."

We soon had ample opportunity to test that declaration!

XXIV

IN THE NAME OF JESUS

The neighbor departed. I sat in stunned silence, still not quite convinced of the authenticity of the "witch."

I puzzled over the matter. The Bible spoke of witches, I reasoned, condemning them to death; so such persons must exist. They seemingly possessed great power, judging from the record of the witch of Endor, who "called up" Samuel at the request of King Saul. But such people were not a reality today, were they?

Dorcas Dewey, the mission nurse, entered the house. "Ginger was here," she announced.

"How'd you know?" Mrs. Thacker asked, turning in surprise from the dishpan.

Dorcas laughed. "Her perfume, dear. No one else wears anything like it." Only then did I notice that faint lingering scent. It disturbed me.

I wanted to ask more about Ginger and her peculiar powers, but hesitated to do so. I waited.

"Say, Brother Eagle," Bud Green spoke suddenly. "If you ever go to Ginger's house and she offers you a cup of tea, don't accept it!"

"Why not?" I asked curiously. "I like tea."

"She has told some people that she puts a potion in it which makes a man helpless," Bud replied. I guess I looked blank. Dorcas enlarged. "He falls hopelessly in love with her."

"You don't believe that!" I protested.

"Brother Eagle," Mrs. Thacker began soberly, "Ginger is a servant of the Devil. We know he has tremendous power. Just how great that power is, few of us realize. Where Ginger is concerned, we take *no* chances!"

"She has 'admirers' who have come to her from as far away as Oregon," Dorcas volunteered.

"But . . ." I stammered doubtfully.

"She belongs to a Lonely Hearts Club," Mrs. Thacker explained. "That accounts for some of them. We're at a loss to explain some others."

". . . and her palm reading and fortune telling," Dorcas added soberly. "That is how she makes her living."

We prayed for Ginger on the spot. As the superintendent read the opening Scripture on Sunday morning, a commotion at the rear of the church caused many people to turn around. Dorcas Dewey, accompanied by scarlet clad Ginger, walked up the aisle to a bench. As she entered, the ladies on the seat edged warily toward the other end. Dorcas sat down next to Ginger.

In a loud whisper, Ginger said, "You're not afraid of me, are you, Dorcas?"

Dorcas squeezed her hand and smiled. "No. I love you, Ginger."

Following the sermon I gave the invitation, inviting anyone who wished to be saved to come forward. Almost to our surprise, Ginger came to the altar. "Oh, Mister, I do want to be saved!" she cried.

Brother Thacker and I, accompanied by Bud, Dorcas and several other Christian people, took Ginger into the prayer room. For two hours we talked to her, assuring her of God's love for her, and of His willingness to forgive her.

"I'm too wicked to be saved," Ginger declared at last. "I've served the Devil too long. I've got all kinds of things to cast spells, and many books of magic. I've gone too far. God can't save me."

The Holy Spirit prompted my memory. "Oh, yes He can," I insisted. "There were people in Paul's day who used magic, too, but Christ saved them. Listen to this." I read from Acts 19, the account of the bonfire at Ephesus, in which the people burned their books of sorcery and magic.

"Shall we have a bonfire at your house, Ginger?" Brother Thacker asked. She agreed and led the way across the road.

Upon entering that house, we found that more than books would need to be destroyed. Pictures of partially clad men and women covered the walls. I began to sense the depth of Satan's grip upon his victim.

As we stood in indecision, not certain how or where to begin, Ginger invited, "Won't you have a cup of tea with me?" and started for the kitchen.

"No thank you, Ginger," Brother Thacker replied. "We have more important things to take care of." He looked about inquisitively. "Where are the books?"

Ginger produced the books. "These pictures ought to go, too, Ginger," I urged, indicating the photographs. Obediently, she began ripping them from the walls. Dorcas and Bud helped. The debris made quite a heap.

"Ginger, is there anything else you should get rid of?" I

asked. "Anything in the old life that would be displeasing to God? That would dishonor Him?"

The woman paused only a moment. "Yes," she confessed. She led the way to a bedside stand and opened a drawer. "I belong to a Lonely Hearts Club. I have letters here from about forty men." She handed me one. "Read it!" she commanded.

It was vile! I read only a brief part of the whole. "Are they all like this?"

"Yes."

Those letters joined the growing rubbish heap.

The letters reminded Ginger of their authors. Reluctantly, she gathered together a handful of photographs of men who had been her lovers. One by one they took their place on the trash pile.

"Oh, Mister," Ginger balked, pausing at one photograph, "I can't throw this one away! He was such a nice man, so good looking, and he was nice, to me, too. I'll keep this one." Her fingers clutched the picture possessively.

"No, Ginger; it will have to go, too," Brother Thacker insisted firmly but kindly.

"Old things must go, Ginger," I elaborated. "The old things that are evil, or remind us of the evil past, must be done away with. That picture would do that. It would make you remember your past sins, and God wants you to forget them because He will, after they are forgiven." Ginger surrendered the photograph.

Another picture arrested her attention. "Do I have to destroy this one?" she cried, displaying the snapshot of a blonde little girl. "My baby girl. She died when she was seven years old," she said.

We assured her she could keep that print.

"Is there anything more that the Lord wants you to dispose of, Ginger?" I asked.

Slowly, her glance swept about the denuded walls. It dropped to the bed. Frantically, she snatched an object from under the pillow and held it determinedly in her hand.

"What is it, Ginger?" I asked forcefully, sensing anew that the enemy wouldn't permit us an easy victory.

Ginger sighed. She gripped the object fiercely. "A charm, to help me sleep at night," she said defiantly. "It cost me $100.00."

I extended my hand commandingly. "Ginger, in the name of Jesus, give that to me. If you have Jesus, you'll be able to sleep. You won't need a charm." She placed it in my hand, a skull and crossbones, made of carved ivory. I broke it to bits and dropped them in my pocket.

I picked up a brown bag tied with a brown shoe string. "What is this, Ginger?"

"Oh, that's the Devil's shoe string."

The bag contained two bottles, one with red liquid and the other with black. "What are these, Ginger?"

"That's Devil's blood," she answered, pointing to the red liquid. "I ordered it from Michigan and sell it for $30 a drop to people who want to put a curse on their enemies."

Without warning, Ginger's eyes became wild and staring. She grabbed the bottle from my hand and fairly ran around the room, uttering blood-curdling screams. Someone in our group started singing, "Power in the Blood." As we sang the chorus, "There is power, power, wonder-working power in the blood of the Lamb . . ." Ginger stopped screaming. We finished the chorus.

"What happened?" our hostess asked wonderingly. "I feel so well now. Something got hold of me."

"It was the power of the evil one, Ginger," I told her. "In the name of Jesus, give me that bottle." Meekly, she handed it to me. I slipped it in my pocket.

Now Ginger noticed the black bottle still in my left hand. She snatched it from me, screeching, "That's my lodestone!" She ran frantically about the room screaming and crying. We began to pray in the name of Jesus and again her sanity returned. At my request, in the name of Jesus, Ginger gave me the bottle of lodestone.

Suddenly Ginger took Dorcas by the hand and examined her palm minutely. She murmured, "Dorcas, you have the lines of a murderer in your hand. If it hadn't been for Jesus, you would have been a murderer."

Stunned, Dorcas Dewey wept. "I've always had a terrible temper," she confessed. She bowed her head and said, "Thank you, dear Father, for Jesus and His salvation."

Now that I had possession of the bottles, I wanted to dispose of them and the charm, as quickly and completely as possible. "Brother Thacker," I suggested, "why don't you and Bud burn this pile of stuff while I take care of these bottles?" They agreed.

I returned from my mission a few minutes later to find a roaring fire. We watched triumphantly as the flames devoured the works of Satan.

"If you want to serve the Lord, Ginger," Dorcas said gently

as we went back to the house, "you shouldn't wear scarlet clothing."

"But I'll look old in blue or green!" Ginger wailed in dismay.

Perhaps it was cruel, but I picked up a hand mirror and gave it to her, remarking, "You already do, Ginger." You know, when we serve the Devil long enough, we get to look like him, and she did.

In spite of the tremendous power Christ had exhibited that day, Ginger remained unwilling to yield fully to Him. The enemy won a temporary victory.

However, Brother Thacker had learned a valuable truth. "I never realized the name of Jesus has such power!" he marvelled.

It was my first collision, but by no means my last, with the openly demonic forces of Satan. At that time I had no inkling of God's purpose in bringing me face to face with this situation. I had no way of knowing then that I would face it again, in many different forms, in the Northland.

XXV

THE LOST FOUND

"Here is a letter from Brother Allen and Betsy," Susie said upon my return from Kentucky. It had been sometime since we had heard from Allen, and I read the letter eagerly.

"Opportunity has come to expand the work; we have enlarged our field of service. Since all of the Indian tribes with which we were working were in Canada, and due also to the International boundary, we have shifted our center of operation for the Canadian work to Red Lake, Ontario, a small mining village in northwestern Ontario. Here already the Lord has opened doors. We serve several bush stations which must be reached by plane. I now have my pilot's license and do some flying in addition to administrative work."

I glanced at my wife and grinned. "Allen Martz piloting a plane?" I quipped. "Can you imagine it?"

Susie smiled. "I've heard of stranger things, dear. We don't know what the Lord may have in store for us yet," she warned.

I read further, "Betsy and the children are still living in Minnesota so that the children won't need to change schools. I drive home to be with them over weekends. They will join me for the summer in Red Lake, once school is out. I'm looking forward to their arrival, although our living quarters here at Red Lake are rather poor at present."

Allen's letter shifted to other difficulties. "Airplane repairs are a big problem here. Because Red Lake is so small, we have no plane repair shop. All repairs must be done in the States which is very expensive and time-consuming. Although I'm certainly no mechanic, I have been able to handle many small repair jobs myself." I marvelled at Allen's versatility.

That same day another letter arrived, asking me to hold a series of meetings in Newport News, Va. I agreed. The services were to begin on Sunday night, October 31. I planned to leave on Saturday morning in order to allow plenty of time for the journey.

As the time of departure approached, doubts filled my soul. I had enough money for gas for the trip, but Susie also needed groceries. If I gave her grocery money, I wouldn't have enough left for traveling expenses. I was in a real bind; I didn't know what to do.

I began praying, which, by the way, is what I should have been doing sooner. "Lord, I can't go," I began, and went on to tell the Lord why I couldn't go. "If I give Susie money for groceries, I won't have enough for gas. If I keep enough for gas, she won't have any for groceries." An inner resolve turned into faith. I went on, "But Lord, I'm going anyway. I'll leave Susie enough money for groceries. I'll take just enough to get some gas and trust you to supply the rest." Peace filled my mind. The Lord had never failed us in the past, nor would He now.

Susie packed my bag. I bid my family good-bye and walked toward the door of our hill home. As my hand touched the doorknob, someone on the outside knocked on the door. I opened it to find three brethren from down country standing there.

"We were in the neighborhood on business and decided to drop in," they stated.

The older of the three men noted my suitcase. "Oh, you're all packed up," he said. "Where are you heading?"

"I'm going to Newport News, Virginia, for a series of meetings," I replied. "Won't you come in and sit down?"

"No," they graciously declined. "We won't detain you." The spokesman put his hand into his pocket and extracted a green bill, which he slipped into my coat pocket. His two companions did the same. Awe-struck at my Lord's faithfulness and provision for us, I thanked them, wished them the Lord's blessing, and they departed.

When I removed the bills, I held $35.00 in my hand. I shared with my wife and began my journey, determined to trust my Heavenly Father more fully than I ever had before. And in all the years since that day, never once has the meal in the barrel wasted or the oil been stayed.

The Lord proved His faithfulness in another area. My soul remembered with deep yearning the old Bible of home. Even now, I found it difficult to reconcile myself to its loss. It would have added so much to my home, if only . . .

Then, one day it happened!

Three weeks after my return from Newport News, I left home for a week of meetings at Rutgers, a small church about thirty miles from Stoneburg.

It wasn't a large congregation. As I stood before them on Sunday morning, I scanned the eager faces of the listening audience. A group which appeared to be one large family impressed me. They stuck out like the proverbial "sore thumb."

This family, with their shabby, well-worn garments, and the boys' hair, on which a cutting was considerably overdue, reminded me so much of the one from which I had come. My heart went out to them.

To my utter surprise and delight, after the services they warmly invited me to their home for dinner.

"It won't be anything fine," Sister Dean explained, "But you're more than welcome." Strange, and yet wonderful! Although I soon had a number of other invitations to dinner that day, I later found it providential that I had received theirs first and accepted it.

Much to the embarrassment of my host, Brother Dean's ancient car balked and refused to start when we were ready to leave the church. I pushed it off on the slightly downward grade and hopped in the front seat beside him and two of the boys, as the motor coughed, sputtered, and turned over. Amid much cheerful conversation in the packed car we drove to the Dean home.

More memories of my own childhood flooded my mind as we entered the front door of that old house. A burst of warmth greeted us from a pot-bellied stove in the living room. At my feet a neatly braided rag rug covered the linoleum. That carpet looked so well worn, I wondered if there might not be a jagged hole in the linoleum beneath that handmade rug. (There had been at our house, I recalled!)

My eyes took in more details of the room. Could that possibly be it? In the center of the table an old family Bible lay open.

"That is a beautiful Book," I remarked, walking casually over to the battered table to examine it.

"I bought it for $1.50 at a sale," Brother Dean replied.

I ran my finger down the front cover. Sure enough! there it was—that v-shaped wedge chipped in the hard cover near the bottom! I checked other identifying marks—the color picture of Daniel in the lion's den that Vernon had torn; the smudged finger prints that Ellen had left on the painting of Baby Jesus; the happy teardrops Mother had spilled over Psalm 91. They were all there. Not a doubt lingered in my mind. At last I had found Mother's old family Bible. This heart of mine was so full of joy that some of it condensed and spilled down my face. I wasn't a bit ashamed though, because it was like meeting a long-lost member of the family.

Sister Dean served a simple meal of home-cured ham, greens, potatoes, and fruit. "This dish is delicious," I remarked, tasting the greens. "What is it?"

Candidly Mrs. Dean replied. "Brother Eagle, I didn't have quite enough greens, so I added dry bread crumbs to stretch them. It is a trick my mother taught me. We find it quite tasty."

Again my mind darted back to my boyhood home. "Sister Dean," I said quietly, "my mother often did the same thing. This is the first time since her death that I've tasted anything like it. Thank you for fixing them."

The children helped clear the table, then Sister Dean sat down to read to her family, just as my Mother had often done. Reverent silence filled that room, as the family clustered around her chair to listen.

It was then that I told them the history of their book and of the blessing it had been in our home. One of the children climbed into my lap and I almost thought I saw an angel smile as the tousle-haired four-year-old remarked, "Mr. Preacher, I love to hear my mommy read from your mother's old Bible."

I glanced about at the earnest, bobbing heads of the children. A deep peace settled in my soul. Mother's old family Bible would have a glorious future. I was content.

And surely, if He saw fit, the Lord could find another one to fill that empty spot on the mantel in our little home.

XXVI

NORTHWARD TO RED LAKE

The Lord's "white shirt" revelation to Susie proved to be increasingly true and real.

As time passed, my area of service grew larger. I found myself traveling to many states to hold revival meetings. In the early summer of 1953 I arrived in northern Minnesota for a series of meetings. In addition to those in Minnesota, additional services were scheduled for the return trip at several places in Wisconsin and Ohio.

But the Lord had other plans for me, I discovered. It came about this way.

During my last service at Strawberry Lake, Minnesota, three people caught my attention. Their behavior puzzled me. While their attitude bespoke reverence, their activity during my sermon annoyed me. Their hands and lips moved constantly. I couldn't reconcile their reverent attitude with all this activity.

Following the service, Linden Gray asked, "Did you notice the interpreters interpreting the message while you spoke, Brother Eagle?" He continued, "We had three different tribes of Indians present tonight, none of whom spoke English. Fortunately, someone from each tribe understood enough to be able to transpose for the others."

Heartily ashamed of my annoyance, I replied, "So *that's* what was going on! I couldn't figure it out. I must confess that I found it very annoying."

Brother Gray nodded. "I'm sorry, Brother Eagle. I should have prepared you beforehand. I knew this could happen."

He stood silently, evidently deep in thought. His next words startled me.

"Brother Eagle, we want you to go north while you are here. We want you to go up to Red Lake to preach for the missionaries in the work there, and also to the native people."

Thunderstruck, I considered quickly. I had a preaching appointment in Wisconsin the next evening. I couldn't possibly drive to Red Lake, or fly, for that matter, to preach to the people there, and get back to my Wisconsin appointment in time. I said so. "I'm sorry, Linden," I said, "but I've promised to preach in several places in Wisconsin and Ohio on the way home.

I don't see how I can do it."

The congregation had departed. The small church stood empty, except for the two of us. Linden Gray looked at me with eyes that pierced my soul. "Which are the more important, Kenneth?" he asked, "the few who can't get anyone to bring the Gospel to them, or the many who can get anyone they please?"

The answer to that came easily and I walked right into the trap! "Why, the few who can't get anyone!" I replied.

"That's right!" Linden Gray answered firmly, "and tomorrow you're leaving for the Northland!"

Just that simply, the decision that has changed my entire life was made for me. However, at the time, I was totally unaware of its far-reaching implications.

Accordingly I phoned to the various pastors in whose churches I had agreed to speak, canceling my engagements, and prepared to leave for Canada the next day.

Don Driver, another local pastor, joined us for the trip north. We drove for several hours before arriving at International Falls, Minnesota. I watched, fascinated, as Don followed the signs pointing out the route which would take us across the border into Canada. The road meandered briefly through the town, then made a sharp right-hand turn. We now faced a narrow metal bridge which spanned the Rainey River, the official boundary line between the nations at this point.

Every vehicle entering Canada must report to the customs officials at the office adjacent to the bridge. Linden Gray, who had crossed the line previously on several occasions, anticipated no difficulties.

The customs official eyed us coldly. "Where are you going in Canada?" he snapped.

"We're going up to Red Lake," Don replied.

"Who are you and where are you from?" he shot back suspiciously, surveying our garb critically. I examined my white shirt, wondering what about our manner of dress could have caused such animosity in our antagonist.

"We're ministers—preachers of the Gospel," Linden Gray answered from his side of the car. He enlarged, giving our names and addresses.

"Oh! You won't get away with that one," the customs man declared. "I've heard it before! Can you prove you're ministers? Do you have your ordination certificates, or anything else that will identify you as ministers? Let me see them!"

Flabbergasted, Linden Gray glanced questioningly at Don and me. "I'm sorry, sir," he said, "but we don't have the certificates with us. We had no idea that we would need them."

"That's a likely story," the agent accused. "Communist agents generally tell us that they are religious people. That is how they enter our country." He stood up and added firmly, "I'm sorry."

What were we to do now? Here we were, inside the Canadian border, but blocked from going further by an official who was thoroughly convinced that we were communist agents posing as preachers. I was praying for direction and I'm sure that Driver and Gray were doing the same. Something prompted me to say, "We're going north to preach to the Indians at Red Lake, up where Allen Martz and the Mennonites are working."

Immediately the man's expression changed. "Oh, that's different!" he declared. "I'm a Christian, too—a Missionary Alliance man. Those men at Red Lake are doing a great work. The Lord bless you!" and he motioned for us to proceed. We drove north, marvelling at how the Lord had interceded in our behalf.

The road took us through some of the most extraordinary country I had ever seen. Beautiful lakes; gray poplars and white birch; tall pines and spruce, many festooned with dirty, moldy looking moss; areas of bogs and marshes where trees stood stark, naked, dead—killed by that same gray fungus. The road dodged between and around huge granite outcroppings of an amazing variety of colors. Flowers of many colors grew plentifully beside the road. At one point, Rushing River cascaded over the rocks, forming enchanting rapids. How I wished Susie and the children could have been with me to share the joys of this fascinating country!

We left the hardsurfaced road at Vermillion Bay. For the next 110 miles, the last lap of the journey, the road would be unpaved. In fact, the Red Lake area had been opened to commercialization only fairly recently. This road had been built in 1948, just five years before.

Red Lake village sprawled along the edge of the water. It reminded me of an American frontier town as it might have appeared fifty years ago; Indian pedestrians and dogs were everywhere. The road petered out among the squalid buildings edging the lake. For once in my life I had literally come to the end of the road!

Fellowshipping with Allen and Betsy Martz was a real joy. We stood in their makeshift home that was perched on a knoll overlooking Red Lake, and watched the gulls coming and going. Their white wings against the blue water formed a lovely contrast to the squalor of the town.

The birds reminded me of flying. "Where do you have your plane?" I asked.

"The plane and supply truck are out at Sand Beach, several miles from here," Allen replied. He grinned quietly, "I lived in the truck until I could get this house in shape to move into."

Allen changed the subject abruptly. "I sent for you, Kenneth, because our workers in the bush need the encouragement of other believers. If you can be ready, I'll fly you in to Popular Hill in about an hour," he stated. "Jim Byler is there alone right now, although the Brunks should be back shortly. I know Jim will be glad to see you." Allen's eyes smiled as he added, "I think you'll profit from meeting Jimmie, too, Kenneth."

"I'm ready at any time, Allen; I'm at your service," I reminded him with a grin. "Am I safe in flying with you?"

"What do you think?" he shot back smilingly.

"Have you had any accidents?" I asked Allen as we drove over the sandy road toward the beach and the mission plane.

"Yes." He looked at me crookedly and smiled. "Remind me to tell you about it when we have more time." He drew the car up to a flat stretch of sandy beach. A small, single-engine plane floated lazily in the faintly brown-tinged water. A truck was parked nearby.

Allen took a gadget from the truck and sucked the moisture from the pontoons which held the plane afloat. As he did so, he informed me, "In the winter, these pontoons are removed and the plane is fitted with skis to land on ice."

"What do you do when emergency repairs are necessary?" I asked, recalling the small, nondescript town. Now, after seeing the place, I understood why plane repairs would not be available here!

Allen paused in loading the plane to smile soberly. "It depends upon what you consider an emergency, Kenneth. If it isn't too serious, I try to do it myself. Of course, if I can't handle it, it goes back to the States."

"But what do you do for transportation while you're waiting for the repairs to be made?" I asked wonderingly.

"Pay a commercial plane to carry our supplies to the bush," Allen replied ruefully.

"Isn't that terribly expensive?" I asked, handing Allen a box of cereal, which he tucked into a convenient corner of the tail of the plane.

"Yes, and not always dependable," he grinned. I sensed a story and waited. "Sometime ago our plane was out, so I asked the local company to fly supplies out to Poplar for Jimmie. They forgot them, and it was three weeks before we found out about it. Jimmie ran out of food and lived on fish during that time. He ate fish for breakfast, dinner, and supper."

As I considered that diet, Allen continued, "Plane repairs have been one of our biggest expenses. If we had a mechanic here who could do the work for us . . . But airplane mechanics are precious, and one who would be willing to come to a place like this . . . Well . . ."

Mentally I decided that my God was big enough to supply even this need, which seemed legitimate to me. I made it a point of prayer as I deposited my suitcase on top of the odds and ends that filled the back of the plane and climbed in after it. Surely, I thought as I settled into my seat next to Allen, somewhere among the men of the church there must be at least *one* whom the Lord could use to meet this need.

Allen glanced back over our heavily loaded plane. "Operating this craft is expensive," he said as he taxied out into the lake. "We like to make a trip into the bush worthwhile when we go."

I noted the island lying below me and fingers of Red Lake leading off in various directions as the plane left the water, banked sharply, and circled northward. I glanced down to see small bleak Indian houses bordering the lake shore out beyond the village limits. Huge power lines cut through the timber to the mines surrounded by an endless expanse of bushland cluttered with lakes, rivers, and muskeg. In some places only sparse vegetation existed, due to large outcroppings of pink-hued ledges.

The ninety-mile trip to Poplar Hill required approximately one hour. As we taxied up to the dock in front of a neat log dwelling, a small, wiry, dark-complexioned, black-haired youth dropped his axe and came to meet us. Smiling broadly, he pulled the craft in to dock and tied it securely.

"Good morning, Jimmie," Allen smiled, stepping from the plane to the dock.

I alighted gingerly. Brother Allen introduced Jimmie and me to each other. A wide grin creased the youth's face. I liked him immediately.

"I've brought Brother Eagle out to spend some time with you," Allen explained. "How does that sound to you, Jimmie?"

"Wonderful!" Jimmie beamed. Turning to me, he said, "We really get starved for fellowship sometimes, Brother Eagle."

"How is the work going, Jimmie?" Allen asked, as we left the dock and walked toward the cabin, each carrying a box of supplies from the plane.

Jimmie paused on the porch. "Allen, our counsellor here has been changed," he said slowly. "You know that Dave was always very cooperative. Jay Meekis has replaced him, and he is very anti-gospel. He's giving me a rough time."

"The counsellor is the native tribal leader," Allen explained to me.

He turned to Jimmie, "We'll be praying," he promised, and walked toward the dock. He waved as the plane taxied away from the dock and out into the lake.

Jimmie welcomed me into his bush home. I looked around that cabin, marvelling at its simplicity. All of the furnishings, with the exception of stoves, cooking utensils, and kerosene lamps, were hand made. Of course, I mused when I had paused to consider, how could it be otherwise? There were no hardware stores in the bush where furniture could be purchased. Everything here must be transported by plane, or made on the spot. When this sank in, I began to wonder how the cook stove had been brought in. It was too bulky to carry in the small mission plane.

"Oh," Jimmie grinned when I voiced the question, "we took it apart to fly it in, then bolted it back together after we had all the pieces." I shook my head in wonder.

"Jimmie," I said, "how do you happen to be serving here in the north?"

"I came west to Minnesota to teach Bible School last summer," Jimmie told me. "I learned that teachers were needed for a school at Pikangikum, another one of our bush stations. So I came to help there. Allen asked me to stay. I plan to take time off soon to get my pilot's license."

"You enjoy flying?" I asked, noting the twinkle in Jimmie's dark eyes.

"Well, here in the north, it is a necessity," he stated, swatting a hungry mosquito which had settled on his arm. He laughed heartily; I sensed a story and eased back in my chair, prepared to enjoy it to the fullest.

"Did you notice all that water beneath you as you flew out?" Jimmie asked.

"Yes," I nodded, adding, "if a plane had to come down, it looks as if the pilot ought to be able to land on water; there is so much of it."

Jimmie's smile deepened. "So I thought, too," he replied. "Unfortunately, it doesn't always work out that way!"

XXVII

THE CRY OF THE NORTHLAND

I re-echoed Jimmie's words. "Unfortunately, it doesn't always work out that way!" What did he mean? Had he been in a plane crash? Had the mission suffered any casualties? I knew of none. Allen Martz's "remind me to tell you about it sometime" flashed into my mind.

"How did it happen, Jimmie?" I asked, hunching forward in my chair. My ears must have stood straight out, I was so curious.

"During my first trip to Red Lake," Jimmie began, "Brother Allen was bringing a load of supplies in to Pikangikum. He had invited an Indian lad along as a passenger to assist in interpreting the Indian language. However, the load was too heavy and he couldn't take off." Jimmie grinned broadly and continued. "He taxied up to the dock and looked me over. 'You're not so big,' he said. 'Why don't I take you?' I took the Indian's seat, and we started out. We succeeded in getting airborne, but we hadn't gone far when the engine lost power. Brother Allen tried to turn the plane to bring it down to the lake, but we'd lost too much altitude."

I was sitting on the edge of my chair in suspense. "What happened, Jimmie? You're both alive and well, I notice!"

Jimmie laughed with me. "The plane came down over the timber, ripping the pontoons completely off as it hit the water. It landed in the lake. Interestingly enough, neither Allen nor I could swim!"

"What did you do?" I gasped.

"Well, Allen managed to get out quickly, since he was accustomed to operating the seat belts, but I couldn't get the clasp loose on mine," Jimmie replied. "The plane kept settling lower and lower and lower in the water while I kept yanking at the buckle of the seat belt. I think," Jimmie elaborated, "that in my haste, I was tightening it, rather than loosening it. The water in the plane inched upward. I raised my chin higher and higher," he demonstrated, tilting his head backward with chin jutted upward and forward, "to keep my nose out of the water. But still I couldn't budge that clasp. Finally, I was completely submerged. 'Well, Lord,' I said, 'I'm coming home sooner than I expected to.'" But the clasp gave and I floated to the surface. The first thing I saw was Brother Allen with those beautiful orange life preservers under his arm. They really looked good!''

"I'll bet they did!" I echoed, shaking my head in wonder.

"I clambered out of the plane and we sat on the wing of the plane to put the life preservers on. We perched there, trying to decide what to do next. That was decided for us when Allen's leg broke through the fabric of the wing. We knew we'd have to get to the island, although neither of us could swim." Jimmie's eyes twinkled. I knew that more followed. I waited.

"We dropped off the wing, into the water. We kicked and floundered, trying to get to shore, but our life preservers began to take on water. Allen kicked off his shoes and trousers. He took his bill fold, which contained all the money he had, and put it in his mouth to carry it. I removed my shoes, too. Soon, Allen had to spit the bill fold out because his mouth got too full of water." A sudden mental picture of those two hapless men flashed into my mind and I laughed aloud. I realized at once that the experience really hadn't been funny, and I apologized.

Jimmy laughed. "That's all right, Brother Eagle. Since it is over, we can see the humor, too; Allen and I still joke about it."

"What did you do? How did you get to shore?"

"We just told the Lord He'd have to help us if He had something more for us to do," Jimmie answered. "Somehow, we made it."

"But even then," he continued, "we were stranded. Our transportation, and all of our financial resources, lay at the bottom of the lake. Added to that, the loss of the plane put the future of our missions in the north in serious jeopardy. We felt very much alone," Jimmie said. "In fact, Allen said he felt like John on the isle of Patmos!"

"How did you get back?"

Jimmie chuckled. "We were a sight, Brother Eagle. Neither of us was fully clothed. The mosquitoes about ate us up. The ants crawled over our bare feet and nearly drove us wild. We had to do something! I climbed a tree to look for a boat. Fortunately, one was anchored across the bay. I pulled off my tee shirt and waved it to attract their attention. These men picked us up and took us back to Sand Beach. Of course, the truck was there, and we were able to drive back to Red Lake."

I sat thoughtfully, pondering the predicament of my two friends. I voiced my question, "If Allen had no clothing and no money, what did he do? He had to get trousers somewhere!"

Jimmie nodded. "Elsie Reinbold was helping in the work at that time, and she had enough money to replace Allen's trousers.

The plane was a different matter."

"How did you replace it?"

"A brother in Pennsylvania donated one exactly like the one we lost. We praised the Lord for it."

"Did you ever recover the wrecked one?" I asked curiously.

"Oh, yes," Jimmie answered, "But very little value remained to it."

We sat in silence a few minutes. Jimmie reverted to the original thread of his story. "It was as we were returning to Kenora, following this experience that Brother Allen asked me why I had to return home. By this time," Jimmie said with a grave smile, "I was fully convinced that the call I had just heard was from the Lord. I stayed."

Jimmie and I sat on the porch in the late Canadian evening. It was after 9 p.m. but still light. The quiet peace of the bush caressed us. Only the hum of an outboard motor on the lake disturbed the silence.

The boat hummed to a halt at our dock. Jimmie glanced in that direction. Visibly, his entire body tensed. The muscles in his face tightened; his lips grew taut. Silently I wondered whom the approaching Indian could be and why this appearance should produce this effect in my young friend. The Indian toted an outboard motor.

"Boosho,"* the Indian greeted Jimmie.

"Boosho," Jimmie returned, trying to reply naturally and cheerfully, but his effort appeared strained.

The visitor and Jimmie conversed briefly. I understood nothing of the conversation since they spoke in the Indian dialect used in the area. True, Jimmie's part of the conversation had been hesitating and halting, but to me his progress with the language seemed phenomenal.

Motioning for me to follow, Jimmie and the Indian walked around to the back of the cabin. Together they tinkered with the motor until they had it running. The Indian departed, without a word of gratitude that I could discern.

"That was Jay Meekis, one of the tribal leaders," Jimmie elaborated. "I really have a tussle where he is concerned. I hate to see him come. My first thought is usually, 'What does he want this time?' I ought to see his visit as an opportunity to witness. Frankly, I just don't like the man!"

I hunted for the right words. While I prayed and thought it over, Jimmie continued, "You know, Brother Eagle, this bothers

* *An Indian term of greeting*

us a lot, too. Did you notice that Jay showed absolutely no appreciation for my help?" I nodded. "The Indians just naturally help each other when they are in need. We find their lack of expressed gratitude quite frustrating; to them, we are only being neighborly, which according to their culture we should be—Christian or not!"

"I think I understand, Jimmie," I answered. "In other words, you are inclined to expect the Indian to respond to your message because of your good deeds, but because of his higher standard of brotherhood, your good deeds lose their—their value."

"You've put it nicely," Jimmie responded. "For example: Last winter I killed a moose. By the way," he interrupted himself, "this will be an illustration in reverse." He continued, "We needed the meat, so we felt justified in keeping it. This really caused hard feelings. The Indians always share their meat among themselves, and here we, who are children of God, who teach love and concern for others, and who declare loudly that our God will supply our needs, refused to share our meat." Jimmie shook his head sadly. "I think we learned something. Probably, had we been willing to share, the Indians would have given to us in return."

"We'll be praying for you and all the workers, Jimmie," I assured him. "There is victory in Christ in all things, even in this, if we just claim it, through obedience to the Holy Spirit and the Word." I asked, "How is the language coming?"

Jimmie grinned in the gathering dusk. "Slowly," he replied, "slowly." He chuckled. "You spend hours working up a short message and try to find words to fit it. You think you have it right, and then you make a big blunder. The other Sunday I found that I had told the people that the streets of Heaven were made of gold watches!" We laughed together, and Jimmie said, "The older people are very patient. They'll sit for hours, trying to help. As for us, we mustn't mind being laughed at while we're learning the language. We make some pretty rare mistakes!"

I could believe that.

Together, Jimmie and I moved indoors. I recited Psalm 91, a passage which was precious to both of us. We knelt and prayed together over the work of the Lord in the north among the Indian people. We prayed for Jay Meekis and Jimmie's problem. Strengthened, we retired for the night.

The Brunk family returned the next day from Stout Lake where they had been conducting Bible School for the children who were with their parents at the fishing camp.

Brother Brunk and I took the mission boat and visited in many Indian homes scattered around the lake. We entered those small log huts, chunked with moss and often panelled with cardboard sheets decorated with labels from tin cans, to sit on a box or our haunches while we chatted with the Indians who sat on the floor. I met my first Indian baby, sleeping contentedly in its tikonogan, or cradleboard, while its mother mixed bannock, or biscuit dough which served as their bread.

The almost complete absence of furniture struck me. No chairs, no beds, just a stove in the center of the cabin, and a small table or stand in the corner which held a water bucket and a few cooking utensils. A box or wooden chest in some homes must have contained extra bedding or clothing, in addition to that which had been rolled up from the floor against the wall, or hung from nails on the wall.

As I studied the tiny dimensions of those cabins, their sleeping arrangements made sense. Instead of a bedstead, a permanent, space-consuming thing, they merely placed several comforters on the floor in the evening and rolled them up against the wall the next morning, freeing the space for family use. "Quite an arrangement," I thought. But I didn't realize then that many Indian babies die of pneumonia from sleeping on drafty floors.

We walked from house to house along the lake, choosing our footing in the squishy sandy soil, and wading through the knee-high grasses bordering the paths. The aroma of smoke from open fires tickled my senses. Brother Brunk pointed to a moose hide draped around a frame to cure beside the open fire. It was an aroma which came to be for me a symbol of the Northland.

We stopped to chat with a wrinkled old man who sat on his doorstep. When we spoke to him of salvation in Christ, he replied, and it wrung my heart, "If these things you say are true, why did you wait so long to tell us? Why didn't you come to us sooner, so that our parents and grandparents could have heard of this Jesus who came to save us?" What could we say?

On Sunday we joined the small congregation at Poplar Hill for worship. The people filled the church with enthusiasm. I watched with interest as the children scuttled about. Their activity seemed to be no source of distraction to the older people.

Questions flowed from the gathering. "Where does the Bible tell us that we should tell others about Jesus?" they asked. "Where does it instruct women to wear the veil? We want to know." Patiently, we answered each question. Dinner time passed, but interest persisted strongly. "Why don't some people want to know about Jesus?" one man asked. Why, indeed? My mind jumped to Jay Meekis, the counsellor. "When can we be baptized?" another wanted to know. Finally, at 3:30 p.m. Brother Brunk closed the meeting, but the Indians would have stayed. They still had questions to which they wanted answers.

"Tell us more," they begged. "We want to know more." One elderly man pleaded, "Send more people to teach us about God and how we can live to please Him."

Brother Brunk sadly told them, "We don't have the men to send."

I considered that and amended his statement. "Tell him that we have the men and we also have the money, but it isn't consecrated." Their pleas echoed in my heart. I cried to the Lord, "Oh, Lord, someone must come and teach these Indians." Everywhere we went, it seemed, we heard that same cry. "Tell us more . . . We want to know more . . ."

I left my heart among the Indians. As I returned to my regular pastorate, and as I travelled about the country in evangelistic work, I carried within me a deep burden for the North. I would awaken in the night to hear the echo, "Tell us more. We want to know more . . ." That cry never slipped far from my mind, and I beseeched the Lord continually to send men to these people who lived with fear, superstition, witchcraft, and Devil worship.

As the Lord so frequently does, he used me to answer my own earnest prayers.

But that story is told in the sequel, *Answering the Cry.*

THE END

Answering the Cry. A sequel to *Cry of the Northland* by the same author. This true story dramatically portrays evangelist Kenneth Eagle's response to God's relentless call to ministry among the Indians in the northern Ontario bush country.

Christian Light Publications, Inc., is a nonprofit conservative Mennonite publishing company providing Christ-centered, Biblical literature in a variety of forms including Gospel tracts, books, Sunday school materials, summer Bible school materials, and a full curriculum for Christian day schools and homeschools.

For more information at no obligation or for spiritual help, please write to us at:

Christian Light Publications, Inc.
P. O. Box 1212
Harrisonburg, VA 22801-1212